STREETCAR SUBURBS

STREETCAR SUBURBS

THE PROCESS OF GROWTH IN BOSTON, 1870–1900

SAM B. WARNER, JR.

ORIGINALLY PUBLISHED BY
HARVARD UNIVERSITY PRESS AND THE M.I.T. PRESS

ATHENEUM   1971   NEW YORK

Published by Atheneum
Reprinted by arrangement with Harvard University Press
Copyright © 1962 by the President and Fellows of Harvard College
All rights reserved
Library of Congress Catalog Card Number 62-17228
Manufactured in the United States of America by
The Murray Printing Company
Forge Village, Massachusetts
Published in Canada by McClelland and Stewart Ltd.
First Atheneum Printing December 1968
Second Printing January 1970
Third Printing October 1970
Fourth Printing June 1971

TO LYLE

PREFACE

CERTAINLY the great fascination of urban study lies in the attempt to discover some order in the vast confusion of the modern city.

Size at close range is one of the signal qualities of a city. Everywhere there are ceaseless rows of structures, big masses at least six times a man's height. The continual confrontation of large objects prevents the visual comprehension of the city and forces the ordinary citizen to think of his environment in terms of his street and his friends, or to think of the city in the terms of the newspaper abstraction, the political unit. This explains why city dwellers cherish a river view, a hilltop, or skyscraper panorama which allows the occasional opportunity to grasp at one time the totality of the city.

The city also presents a spectacle of numberless humanity. More than two hundred years have passed since any American could say he knew the name of every man, woman, and child in his city; more than one hundred years have passed since any American could form a reliable estimate of the lives of and relationships among the thousands of people he saw on the streets and in the offices and stores of his city.

Because of these twin problems of visual and human scale the order of the city can only be comprehended by the process of abstraction. One must leave the view of the individual person, the house, and the street, and turn to the panorama and the map, to gross classifications and formal stylized terms. People must become statistics, classes, occupations, ages, and nationalities. The United States Census describes cities in this way every ten years, and planners, engineers, and sociologists are constantly at work on abstract descriptions of cities. Such abstractions, however, are drawn for limited purposes, and designed to deal with specific problems of the moment. Rare are works like Lewis Mumford's which combine a sense of the totality of the city with an understanding of how it grew.

Today both the past and the future weigh heavily upon the cities of America. The old disorders of the railroad, the mill, the department store, the tenement, and the cottage enmesh the new disorders of the superhighway, the industrial park, the shopping center, the apartment house, and the suburban development. It is the purpose of this book to analyze a period in the history of city building in the hope that the reader can gain some understanding of the nature and organization of the disorders that press upon him. If the city is ever to become susceptible to rational planning there must come to be a common understanding of how the city is built.

A book which attempts to describe city building by combining the fragments of local history with the generalizations of a variety of scholars must necessarily rest upon the assistance of many persons. Some of the research was paid for by a Ford Foundation Fellowship in Metropolitan Studies. John P. Molloy of the City of Boston Building Department; Grace Lawson and her assistants at the Calculating and Clerical Service; the librarians of the Massachusetts State Library, the New England Historic Genealogical Society, and the library of the School of Design, Harvard; Maurice Smith; Arthur Wood; Calvin Burnett; Frieda Kay; and Ellis Levine have lent their skill and in many ways departed from the paths of duty to help me in the process of research and the presentation of the findings.

A number of scholars have given freely of their time and knowledge: Abbott L. Cummings of the Society for the Preservation of New England Antiquities, Eric E. Lampard of the University of Wisconsin, Robert C. Wood of Massachusetts Institute of Technology, and Arthur M. Schlesinger, Sr., and Charles R. Cherington of Harvard University.

During the winter of 1959–60 I had the privilege of reworking my material into its present form under the guidance of Lloyd Rodwin of the Massachusetts Institute of Technology and the Joint Center for Urban Studies of M.I.T. and Harvard. John Gaus and Martin Meyerson of Harvard and the Joint Center both gave their time and experience to careful readings of the manuscript.

To two scholars I owe a special debt. Oscar Handlin directed this study as a thesis and continued a valued adviser through all its later transformations. Lee S. Halprin, a friend and fellow student, by his enthusiasm and detailed criticism spurred the work forward from its first crude draft to its final presentation.

A book of this kind which has been made up out of thousands of fragments and compiled over a number of years inevitably contains errors of detail and citation. I have made every effort to eliminate them but no doubt some remain. I would, therefore, appreciate correspondence from local residents and scholars who find mistakes.

Sam B. Warner, Jr.

March 1962
Cambridge, Massachusetts

CONTENTS

ILLUSTRATIONS

MAPS

CHART

FIGURES

All uncredited pictures were taken by the author during the winter of 1958–59. Unless noted to the contrary all houses in the illustrations were still standing in 1961.

        Twenty-acre estate of Stephen M. Allen, 44 Allandale road, near Centre street, West Roxbury. The house burned in 1889 and was replaced by a new and enlarged building which still stands on the same site. Private lithograph by J. H. Bufford. Courtesy Society for the Preservation of New England Antiquities (S.P.N.E.A.).

        Humphreys street, Dorchester, looking from Dudley street. Dudley street carline in the foreground, late eighteenth century house on the left, and rows of 1890 medium-price two-family houses on the right. Courtesy Metropolitan Transit Authority (M.T.A.).

        Courtesy M.T.A.

STREETCAR
SUBURBS

CHAPTER ONE

A CITY DIVIDED

THE CITY of Boston is old and full of monuments to the past. To visitors it often appears a dowdy repository for some of the nation's early memories. But to those who know it better the city's life has always been one of ceaseless change. The visitor who stops at Paul Revere's house seldom realizes that within thirty years the society that had produced so many revolutionaries was dead. And the local resident who stands before William Lloyd Garrison's well-known statue seldom recognizes that the generation of Bostonians who erected this statue could not bring forth such an uncompromising radical. Boston, like the various societies that made it, has been ever changing, ever in transition. The differences that mark the successive eras have come from the shifting of emphasis from one set of problems to another— from politics to business, from foreign trade to manufacture, from prosperity to depression.

No period in Boston's history was more dynamic than the prosperous years of the second half of the nineteenth century. One of the most enduring of the many transformations of this era was the rearrangement of the physical form of the city itself. In fifty years it changed from a merchant city of two hundred thousand inhabitants to an industrial metropolis of over a million. In 1850 Boston was a tightly packed seaport; by 1900 it sprawled over a ten-mile radius and contained thirty-one cities and towns.

The growth of the city brought other major changes. The old settlement of 1850 became by 1900 the principal zone of work—the industrial, commercial, and communications center of the metropolitan region. At the same time the tenements and old dwellings of the area came to house the lower-income half of the population. Beyond the

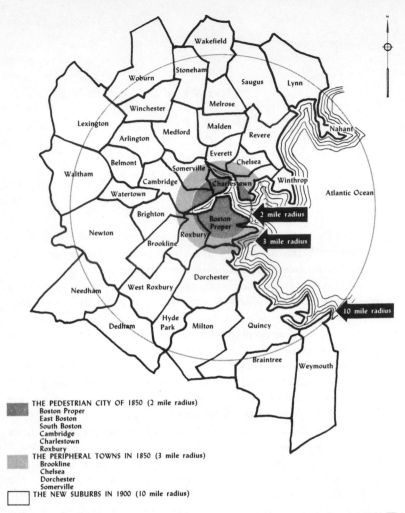

THE PEDESTRIAN CITY OF 1850 (2 mile radius)
  Boston Proper
  East Boston
  South Boston
  Cambridge
  Charlestown
  Roxbury
THE PERIPHERAL TOWNS IN 1850 (3 mile radius)
  Brookline
  Chelsea
  Dorchester
  Somerville
THE NEW SUBURBS IN 1900 (10 mile radius)

MAP 1. The pedestrian city of 1850 and the suburban metropolis of 1900. The metropolis of 1900 is that described by Sylvester Baxter, *Greater Boston; A Study for a Federated Metropolis* (Boston, 1891). See Table 1 for population distribution.

inner concentrated section there grew an equally novel environment, the enormous outer ring of new commuters' houses.

Boston in 1900 was very much a city divided. With the exception of the expensive houses of the Back Bay, it was an inner city of work and low-income housing, and an outer city of middle- and upper-income residences. The wide extent of settlement in the outer residential zone was made possible by the elaboration of the new street railway transportation system, and a parallel extension of city services. Here the course of building reflected the movement of successive waves of people out from the center of the city. Here the new houses and neighborhoods demonstrated the economic progress of half of Boston's families and their aspirations for a satisfactory home environment.

With these changes in scale and plan many of the familiar modern problems of city life began to emerge: the bedroom town; the inundation of country villages by commuters; the sudden withdrawal of whole segments of an old neighborhood's population; the rapid building and rapid decay of entire sections of a city; the spread of the metropolis beyond any encompassing political boundaries; the growth of nonelective agencies of government to meet metropolitan transportation, sanitary, and recreation demands; and, above all, the discipline of the lives of city dwellers into specialized transportation paths, specialized occupations, specialized home environments, and specialized community relationships. With the new metropolis and all its changes the ancient problems of large cities once more came to life: the individual members of urban society became isolated within a physical and social network which had passed their comprehension and control.

In 1850 Boston was something familiar to Western history and manageable by its traditions. The attitudes and institutions that governed its daily life had been developed slowly over at least 500 years. By 1900 it had become, along with many European and American cities, something entirely new, an industrial and suburban metropolis. Most of this metropolis of 1900 still survives. Even today it is the home of the bulk of Greater Boston's industry and commerce, and probably half its population. Decisions made by city officials, corporation managers, and home builders, decisions now sixty to one hundred years old, still rule much of today's social, economic, and political life. Perhaps most important, many of the traditions of thought and behavior first elaborated during the last half of the nineteenth century still dominate present action.

Who Built the Metropolis?

The Boston metropolis is the product of hundreds of thousands of separate decisions. Looking back on the period for which detailed information is available, the years 1870–1900, one can make out a kind of partnership which constructed the new industrial and suburban metropolis. It was a partnership between large institutions and individual investors and homeowners.

No organization, however, tied together the two groups. Boston's water commissioners and the president of the West End Street Railway Company, for example, were guided by their own day-to-day needs. And the homeowner who sought a lot and decided to build a house was unable to change city policy or affect the transportation service currently offered. Although throughout the last half of the nineteenth century one third to one half of the City of Boston's budget was annually committed to projects and services directly affecting real estate, most of the political campaigns turned on other conflicts: Republicans versus Democrats; native Americans versus immigrants; more city jobs versus economy; corruption versus honesty. In addition, no zoning laws and few of the direct regulations now current in American cities then controlled the behavior of builders.

Common ideas and attitudes created the partnership of the large institutions and the individual homeowners and investors. Both groups shared an enthusiasm for a two-part city—a city of work separated from a city of homes. This enthusiasm colored every decision, whether it was a decision made by the director of a large corporation or by a mortgage-pressed carpenter. Both groups were also subject to common disciplines: the disciplines of the contemporary money market, the disciplines of the current engineering and architecture, the disciplines of Boston's geography, and the disciplines of the matrix of prior decisions which set the environment in which men worked.

The building of the new divided metropolis was a popular movement, a movement executed by hundreds of thousands of middle class citizens. This book is a search for the historical background of the multitudes of decisions which together created the new urban environment of 1900. Three questions will guide the search. Who made decisions to build what? What patterns were created by the repetition of individual decisions? What were the consequences of these patterns?

The old records of the building of Boston do not yield information to which a modern sociological class analysis can be applied. Little but the census and legal records survive as the literature of this mass movement. Therefore, the story must be told largely by the patterns made by the end products of the decisions themselves: the parks, the

streets, the pipes, the tracks, the houses. The method of this book will
be to look first at the largest patterns and then with ever narrowing
focus to descend to the smallest patterns. The book will proceed from
common nineteenth century ideas and experiences, to the metropolitan transportation and utility network, to the towns, to the neighborhoods, to single streets, and finally to individual houses and their
builders. In the range of narrow focus Boston's old suburbs, the
formerly independent towns of Roxbury, West Roxbury, and Dorchester, will provide the detail of the story.

COMMON IDEAS AND EXPERIENCES

In the late nineteenth century most Bostonians, indeed most Americans, held in common a certain way of looking at the world. Their
outlook was a product of the conditions of the times. Three sets of
experiences and three associated ideas informed men's life in the city:
The increasing industrialization of work was accompanied by the idea
of romantic capitalism; The experience of immigration gave rise to
nostalgic nationalisms; The impact of ever more intensive urbanization called forth the emotional reaction of the rural ideal. Old residents and newcomers alike interpreted the changing possibilities and
disciplines of their lives in terms of a mixture of these experiences and
ideas.

Industrialization and immigration together fired the economy of
nineteenth century Boston. The port of Boston, one of the most active
ports in the United States, served as the place of entry for thousands
of European immigrants. Prior to the 1840's farmers, artisans, and
millworkers from the British Isles, men squeezed by the shifting
rewards and penalties of English industrialization, made up the bulk
of the new arrivals. Joining them were sizeable numbers of Germans
seeking an escape from the poverty of Central Europe. Also, as the
trading center for New England and the Maritime Provinces of
Canada, Boston attracted a steady flow of men from this back country.

These three main groups of newcomers, though they included small
numbers of German Jews and Irish, German, and French-Canadian
Catholics, were much the same in background, habits, and religion
as the resident population of the city. Indeed, with some variations in
proportions, these areas had supplied New England with its immigrants for the past two hundred years. The strong tide of democratic

tolerance that had been growing since the eighteenth century easily buried such religious and ethnic tensions as existed among these groups, the old residents, and the other small immigrant colonies. Men from the British Isles, from the Maritimes, and from rural New England continued to come to Boston in large numbers throughout the nineteenth century, and with the repeated experience of easy assimilation this immigration came to be fused in people's minds with the old stock.

The great decline of Irish agriculture, beginning with the terrible potato famines of the 1840's, brought a radical change in Boston's population. Catholic Irish peasants, for the most part unskilled and penniless, arrived by the shipload. By 1875, sixty thousand foreign-born Irish were living in Boston. During the balance of the century immigration from that poverty stricken island continued so rapidly that despite the growth of the city the Irish newcomers and their children made up from 30 to 40 percent of Boston's total population. Then, in the last decade of the century, as Irish immigration began to slacken, their place was taken by new waves of people from Central, Eastern, and Southern Europe. Beginning around 1890, Jews and Italians became an important element in the population of the city.

This enormous and continuous influx of people made Boston a great labor pool. Early industrialists had set up their factories in the small towns of New England not only for water power but also to tap the surplus labor resources of the farm—young women and children. Now next to a fully developed seaport there existed a whole army of men and women desperately in need of work. The industrial prosperity of the Boston region dates from the 1840's when improvements in steam engines provided the power, and the flood of cheap labor provided the hands to tend factories and machines. Ironworks, textile and shoe factories, and almost every kind of manufacture came to be carried on in the area. In some cases businessmen adapted old trades to the unskilled peasants. For example, by the Civil War Boston led the nation in the production of inexpensive ready-made garments. Ready-made clothes was a new industry developed by the novel breakdown of tailoring into its simplest operations. With this reorganization unskilled women and children could work this formerly complicated trade in sweatshop factories or tenement homes.

With its old merchant capital and new abundance of workers, the city grew, and grew wealthy, as never before. The money of this period paid for the expensive homes of the South End and Back Bay, the estates of Roxbury, Jamaica Plain, Brookline, Milton, and Dedham. Municipal enterprise went forward on an unprecedented scale. The streets were widened, marshes filled and hills leveled, parks laid out, and miles of waterworks constructed. Year after year the City of Boston's expenditures exceeded those of the Commonwealth of Massachusetts. And the ample stone churches which still stand in every section of the city bear testimony to the wealth of private subscription.

This whole fifty-year era brought with it a special kind of life. Its dynamism and prosperity not only made its economic system of capitalism popular but also generated a kind of enthusiasm for wealth and productivity which gave contemporary enterprise a romantic quality. For the majority of men prosperity and happiness in this capitalist era required the acceptance of its three disciplines: hard work, thrift, and education. Each one of these disciplines was at once a description of rational behavior necessary for the success of the economic system and a prescription of an ideal in its own right.

Hard work and devotion to the task brought advancement in the job and security against being laid off. By long hours, too, ambitious men working on borrowed capital pitted their time against the risks of speculation. Beyond such rational guides to behavior emphasis also fell on hard work because the job lay at the core of romantic capitalism. In this society work was a source of joy as well as a virtue. The society had a great appreciation for productivity in any form. The man whose dozen garish barn signs brought orders for a carload of patent medicines, the inventor of an automatic oven that sent forth an unceasing parade of soda crackers, or the traditional artisan whose high skill and patience could make a violin—all were heroes. However, since the production of personal wealth brought the greatest power in the society, this kind of productivity brought with it the greatest popular standing.

Thrift was likewise a rational economic necessity and a generalized virtue. By putting aside earnings a man could protect himself against hard times, and by thrift he could put himself into a position to buy a business or make some investment. By practicing thrift, just as by working hard, a man also demonstrated virtue and gained respect. In this way he at once realized the benefits of social approval and acquired the standing necessary to borrow money from banks and private investors.

Finally, education was both a tool and a source of status and pleasure. At the lowest level the new industrial society created jobs that needed workers who could read, write, and do arithmetic. The well-paid and rewarding jobs in law, engineering, finance, and business increasingly required educated men who could handle words, numbers, and ideas. With the elaboration of the society and its tools, high school, technical school, and even college and professional education became every year more necessary job criteria. In addition education brought social standing, for people tended to associate class with different levels of training and rising scales of financial reward. Finally, education offered the pleasures inherent in being in touch with the world, both past and present. These pleasures were open alike to the dirt farmer who first learned to read the newspapers, and the college graduate who could follow world literature and technology.

For the average Boston family the formula of hard work, thrift, and education meant a 48- to 55-hour work week for the father, little vacation for the family, and emphasis on the education of the children and financial gain. The ultimate test of the family's success and the key to its social standing rested within the capitalist framework—how much money did the family have, how much property did it control? To have such goals, and to live such a life, was, in the nineteenth century, to be a middle class American.[1]

Such goals were generally shared in the society, as can be seen by the rapid multiplication of stores and businesses; the increase in home-ownership; the frequent use of the words "middle class" as a term of wide inclusiveness; the constant repetition of capitalist goals in popular literature; and, in family histories and reminiscences, the almost universal description of success by thrift, hard work, and education. Perhaps 60 percent of Boston's population was middle class by living habits and aspirations. The exceptions to the dominant code of behavior were some of the rich for whom money making no longer appeared a satisfying way of life, and a large proportion of the lower-income groups for whom wealth was an impossibility.[2]

Another test of the extent to which a society is middle class is to examine the distribution of income. As one might expect, more people held middle class aspirations than enjoyed the income necessary to live out these ideals. A reasonable guess would be that 40 to 50 percent of the families of Boston were middle class by income. Such people were sufficiently well off to live by the income of one member of the family. This income was secure enough not to be drastically curtailed in times of panic; it provided the family with a safe, sanitary environment; and it allowed the family to dispense with children's work at least long enough for them to finish grammar school. Although but one quarter of Boston's families owned houses in 1900, and for a number of reasons many preferred homes in multiple dwellings, it seems also a fair presumption to say that this 40 to 50 percent of the society accumulated enough capital in its lifetime to be able to choose homeownership instead of tenancy. Since most men's income and capital rose slowly, at any given moment probably not more than half of Boston's middle class earned enough or had saved enough to be able to purchase a home. Thus, any year's potential housing market could not have exceeded one fifth of the total families in the city.[3]

Many aspiring to middle class life lacked the income. These families resorted to multiple employment to achieve their goal. If, when the children were young, husband and wife were lucky and neither fell sick or were unemployed for long, in time the earnings of the children would push the family income into the middle range. For the immigrant family who arrived in Boston without skill or capital this advancement to middle class standing usually took two or three generations. The immigrant's children, educated in the public schools and armed with the skills and goals of the American middle class, were frequently the first to benefit from the chance for advancement offered by the industrial prosperity of the age. The constant rise of great numbers of immigrant families to middle-income jobs and their movement into middle class neighborhoods was taken by contemporaries as testimony to the success of the capitalism of the day and a reassurance of its harmony with the general goals of American democracy.

Although the aspirations and disciplines of romantic capitalism dominated the majority of men's minds there were many Bostonians who lacked this conviction. Perhaps 40 percent of the city's population did not have middle class aspirations. Laborers, factory workers, and new immigrants made up most of this group, but to it must be added artisans, clerks, and skilled mechanics who, though they possessed a fair income, resented the discipline of the industrial world and neither understood nor enjoyed the pleasures of a life devoted to the current definition of "getting ahead." Most of those without middle class aspirations, however, took their opposition not so much as a matter of independent belief, but as a consequence of the unequal distribution of income.

For thousands, perhaps one third of Boston, natives and immigrants alike, life brought only the tensions of too few jobs at too little pay, inhuman work conditions, wage cuts and seasonal layoffs, accidents and disease, and, at times, terrible depressions whose effects public authorities relieved only by the inadequate and inhospitable charity of the city's soup kitchens. These economic tensions and hardships led many lower class Bostonians to attack not the methods of industrialism that caused their suffering, but each other.

Quite different from the case of European cities in the second half of the nineteenth century, the suffering of Boston's poor produced no strong movement for corrective alternatives to the dominant capitalism. Instead, men whose fate rested upon the successful reshaping of society in one country and in one era turned their thoughts back to visions of other places and former times. Large numbers of peasants had been driven by famine and hard times from a society of enduring tradition to the hazards of a new land, new work, and a new society that was itself ever changing. Such men sought an anchor against uncertainty and confusion, they sought a device to lessen the scope of the world and thereby render it more manageable.

Old nationalisms and the maintenance of old ethnic ways offered such a device. Nationalism created in large American cities a temporary refuge in which the world could be thought of as containing only one's own group and "the others"—others of whom one need have no knowledge, for whom one need take no responsibility. Nor was the escape into nationalism limited to immigrants. The native poor of Boston, in competition with immigrants for jobs and sharing with them the penalties of the maldistribution of income, often matched the newcomers in clannishness and frequently confronted them with raw hostility. Their nationalism produced the special political movement known as nativism. From 1854 to 1857, nativists were in control of the state government, and antiforeign, anti-Catholic sentiment remained an active ingredient in state and city politics for the rest of the century.

In 1834 a Charlestown convent was burned; in the 1850's there was a church bombing and anti-Catholic riots; Protestant street gangs, militia, and fire companies fought their Irish Catholic counterparts; and later in the century Jewish families became the objects of Irish attacks. More important than these sporadic outbursts of local violence, the nationalist response to the social stress of immigration and industrial change infected all levels of the society with job discrimination, ethnic politics, and racist stereotypes. The whole spectrum of behavior from the aristocrat's snobbery to the barroom brawl distracted men's attention from the problems of poverty, housing, education, and welfare which severely limited the promise of American democracy.

For most Bostonians nationalism was a passive secondary attitude; the business of making a living and mastering wealth and production occupied their major efforts. For lower class families the retreat into sentimental nationalism provided some temporary relief from the pains of life. For the middle class, both families who had achieved the promise of a competence and those still aspiring to it, sentimental nationalism was a second thought, a set of ideas that filled the vacuum left by their dominant code of capitalist striving. It provided a vehicle for thoughts of love and security which capitalist competition ignored, and it occasionally guided action in areas in which there were no capitalist imperatives.

Much of the nationalism of the nineteenth century was a reaction to the stresses of the present, a longing of both native and immigrant for some "old country" or "old days." The immigrant tended to blur the memory of the clay on his boots with a vision of the rolling green hills of Ireland, or obscure the memory of a broken-down farm with the vision of the forests and shores of Maine or Nova Scotia. Russian Jews, Italians, Germans, Scots, Canadians, Englishmen, and Americans all shared a knowledge of a past era prior to industrialization. As every year went by the reality of the past grew dimmer, and the "old country" or "old days" took on the very qualities that were missing in the modern world. In this blend of fact and fancy, life was less disciplined and more leisurely, and men lived in simple communities where all spoke the same language, went to the same church, and shared a common life. Friends were true and wealth unimportant, the girls prettier and the cooking better, honest craftsmen labored for love to make things of beauty, not cheap machine shoddy, and when a man came home at night it was to a neat cottage and a family of healthy happy children.

The sentimental, backward-looking, quality of the urban nationalisms of the late nineteenth century formed part of a general contemporary reaction to the growing industrial metropolis. In abetting this popular movement nationalism joined a strong and old American tradition—the rural ideal. The rural ideal was an attitude which had always contained the notion of escape from city restraints, organizations, and objects. The city's ways and forms were conceived of as too artificial and of the wrong quality to support a moral life. In opposition to the oppressive modes of social behavior in the city, in the country the church, the village, and the home were to provide the setting for simple gatherings of families and friends on a basis of fellowship and common interest.

The very fact of light settlement assisted in the creation of a moral dichotomy between the city as artificial, incomplete, and temporal, and the country as simple, full, and timeless. The wild surroundings of forest, rivers, and hills, like the landscape of farms where men's lives depended directly upon plants and animals, provided some of the key weapons of the rural ideology. Here, the physical setting encouraged the family to live by some concept of harmony with the unending cycles and seasons of nature.

The city, on the other hand, was thought to be the home of feasts and orgies, of clothes cut to fashion alone, of men and women devoting their lives to the pursuit of money, power, and happiness in a setting not made in the image of nature but by the goals of the city itself. Whereas in the country simple village institutions would suffice to police the actions of the villagers, the city often appeared out of control. The city accumulated great wealth, but it seemed lacking in devices to harness that wealth to moral ends.

Fig. 1. A romantic cottage, West Roxbury, 1856–1857

Fig. 2. The suburban achievement, 1903

The prevalence of this contrast between city and country goes far back in the Western world, at least to Roman times. It was, however, the model of the country gentleman of seventeenth and eighteenth century England that transmitted the rural philosophy to the United States. By his service to the state and frequent trips to London the model country gentleman kept his contact with the largest world of his day while at the same time living a well-rounded life on his estate. The lives of the Virginia presidents of the United States were but domestic copies of this image. Men like Harrison Gray Otis and John Hancock, with their town houses and country estates, served as models for middle class Bostonians.

Numerous wealthy families during the first half of the nineteenth century copied this form of life. In Roxbury, West Roxbury, and Dorchester rich men, following the Roman and English traditions of an interest in farming, carried on important experiments in scientific agriculture. Today the remainder of their tradition still survives in the institutions they founded: the Massachusetts Horticultural Society, and the Arnold Arboretum of Harvard University.

Prior to the steam railroad and street railway two houses, not one, were generally required. Just outside Boston, country villages like

Watertown, Jamaica Plain, and Brookline provided the sites for the rural ideal, but most early estate owners needed, also, a town house for their business life and social contacts. The streetcar suburb brought with it a whole set of new problems. Much of its success or failure centered around the attempt by a mass of people, each with but one small house and lot, to achieve what previously had been the pattern of life of a few rich families with two large houses and ample land.

For the middle class of the late nineteenth century the rural ideal was one positive element in a complex of conditions which shifted people's attitude from being favorable to being hostile to city life. The physical deterioration of old neighborhoods, the crowding of factory, shop, and tenement in the old central city, the unceasing flow of foreigners with ever new languages and habits—these negative pressures tended to drive the middle class from the city. The new technology of the street railway and the contemporary sanitary engineering enabled these families to move out from the old city boundaries into an expanded area of vacant and lightly settled land. In this new land the rural ideal, by its emphasis on the pleasures of private family life, on the security of a small community setting, and on the enjoyment of natural surroundings, encouraged the middle class to build a wholly new residential environment: the modern suburb.

CHAPTER TWO

THE LARGE INSTITUTIONS

AT ANY given time the arrangement of streets and buildings in a large city represents a temporary compromise among such diverse and often conflicting elements as aspirations for business and home life, the conditions of trade, the supply of labor, and the ability to remake what came before.

The physical plan of metropolitan Boston in 1850 rested upon a primitive technology of urban transport: Boston was a city of pedestrians. Its form reflected a compromise among convenience and privacy, the aspirations of homeownership, and the high price of land. The arrival of the street railway freed the elements of the compromise from their former discipline of pedestrian movement and bound them together again by its own new discipline. By 1900 the transformation of Boston had been completed. The patterns made by this new compromise are what today is recognized as the suburban form of the metropolitan city.

THE WALKING CITY

In 1850 the area of dense settlement hardly exceeded a two-mile radius from City Hall. It included only portions of the towns and cities of Boston, Brookline, Cambridge, Charlestown, Chelsea, Dorchester, Roxbury, and Somerville. Before the invention of the telephone in 1876 and the introduction of street railways in the 1850's, face-to-face communication and movement on foot were essential ingredients of city life.

One can only guess just how large metropolitan Boston would have grown had there been no invention of new communication devices. If the spread of the city had begun to exceed the distance a man might walk in about an hour, say a three-mile radius, the shops and offices of the metropolis would have fallen out of easy daily communication with each other. The result would have been the destruction of a single unified communication network and the development of semi-autonomous subcities which would have had to duplicate many of the services and facilities offered in other parts of the city. One of the principal contributions of nineteenth century transportation and communication technology was to preserve the centralized communication of the walking city on a vastly enlarged scale.

In 1850 carriages were a prominent sight on Boston's downtown streets. They moved only a small proportion of the city's population, however, because few people could afford to maintain a private horse and carriage. The omnibus and the steam railroad were likewise supplements to walking. The omnibus, an urban version of the stage coach, was first introduced in 1826. It moved slowly, held relatively few passengers, and cost a lot. The steam railroad, in operation since 1835, was also expensive and accomplished, during its first fifteen

FIG. 3. An antique omnibus

years, little to change the old pattern of the city. At best it was a limited method of mass transportation. The railroad was fast but its infrequent stops and its single terminal, often located at some distance from passengers' ultimate destinations, prevented it from offering the great variety of choices of entrance and exit that streetcar systems ultimately provided. Prior to the Civil War the principal contribution of the railroad lay in its joining of the port of Boston, with its wharves and warehouses, to the manufacturing and farming towns of New England. The result was to accelerate the industrialization of both the trading center and its hinterland. For residents of the Boston region the railroad simplified business transactions with outlying industrial cities like Lynn and Waltham. The railroad also enabled some men of wealth and leisure to settle permanently at their summer estates which lay in scattered clusters about the hills beyond Boston.[1]

Before 1850 Boston's geography had inhibited easy expansion. Marshes, rivers, and the ocean restricted the paths of pedestrian communication. Boston itself was a rough, hilly peninsula set on the end of a narrow strip of land that connected it to the mainland at Roxbury. In the general area where the wharves now stand, against the eastern and northern part of the peninsula, lay the deep-water harbor. The rest of the peninsula was surrounded by tidal basins and enormous marshes. So confined by the harbor, Boston land had always been expensive, and almost from the beginning of its settlement men cramped for space began damming and filling the marshes and flats, first for commercial, and later for residential, purposes. As the city prospered and housing standards rose, more extensive works became profitable. Hills were leveled and sea walls built. By the 1850's developers had reclaimed the area around Charles street, parts of the North End, and much of the South End,* and had cut down a good deal of Beacon and other hills.

In the succeeding twenty years Boston's two most ambitious land filling schemes were executed: the South End and the Back Bay. The South End was almost completely taken up with houses by 1880; the Back Bay, by 1900. Only the rich and the prosperous segment of the middle class could afford most of the new houses in these sections even though the common design of narrow row houses, three and one-half to four and one-half stories high, required but small parcels of land.[2]

* See Map 3 for sections of Boston.

Under such circumstances speculators turned their attention to land just beyond the main peninsula. What they wanted was property that could be more easily developed and therefore sold at lower prices. The search for cheap land began long before central Boston was filled. In 1804 South Boston was opened as a housing speculation. Its progress remained slow, however, until the 1830's when the growth of Boston created a shortage of land sufficient to persuade people to move beyond the old peninsula and walk the added distance.[3] Similarly, Charlestown, parts of Cambridge, East Boston, and the nearby sections of Roxbury filled up rapidly in the period from 1830 to 1850 when Boston's industrial prosperity and expansion began to make headway.

These peripheral communities were not simple bedroom towns for commuters, not exact early models of the modern middle class residential suburb; rather they were mixed settlements of Boston commuters and local workers. All these communities lay at the edge of the harbor and possessed considerable industrial and mercantile

Fig. 4. Middle class single-family houses of the peripheral towns, c. 1830–1870

Fig. 5. Mid-nineteenth century working class alley housing located to the rear of houses in Figure 4

potential. Charlestown and East and South Boston developed large shipbuilding and wharf facilities, while Cambridge and Roxbury became manufacturing centers.[4] Promoters of these areas, used to the tight scale of the walking city, saw no incompatibility between residences and factories; they wished to re-create the conditions of Boston.

Throughout the tiny metropolitan region of 1850, streets of the well-to-do lay hard by workers' barracks and tenements of the poor; many artisans kept shop and home in the same building or suite; and factories, wharves, and offices were but a few blocks from middle class homes. The wide physical separation between those who could afford new houses and those who could not awaited the expansion of the city that accompanied the introduction of the street railway.

Despite the peripheral towns' imitation of the central city some architectural differences marked the two areas. On the filled land of the main peninsula close copies of the brick London town row house predominated. In the peripheral areas, detached houses, continuations of eighteenth century American wooden construction, were the rule.

These latter structures were often smaller and generally cheaper than their intown opposites. Today, after detached wooden styles have dominated residential fashions for over eighty years, the little wooden houses of South and East Boston appear to be significant alternatives to the brick row house. In the early nineteenth century, however, these houses were but a continuation of old habits. They were the products of a class of people who had yet to earn the wealth, had yet to learn the modes, of city life.

Compared to the enlarged lots, the picturesque houses, and the planted streets of the streetcar suburbs of the last third of the nineteenth century, the architecture of Boston in 1850 was strongly urban. The houses of the central city and the peripheral towns, set as they were on small narrow lots and generally placed against the street, created a town environment of dense settlement. Building in both

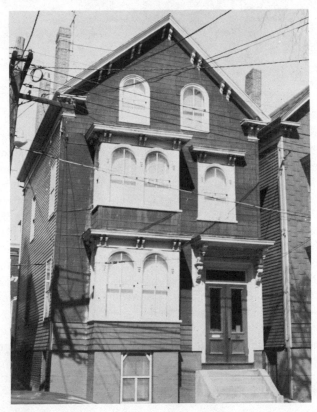

FIG. 6. Medium-priced two-family house, c. 1850

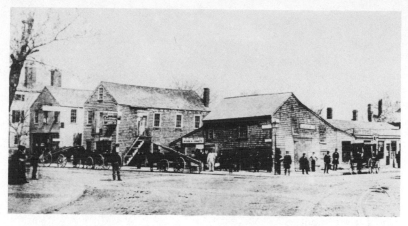

Fig. 7. Roxbury Village, Dudley and Warren streets, c. 1860

areas was eminently suited to a city short of land, a city which depended on people's walking for its means of transportation, a city which depended upon face-to-face relationships as its means of communication.[5]

THE STREET RAILWAYS

The history of Boston's street railways in the nineteenth century is the story of fifty years of aggressive expansion. During both the early years of the horsecar and the later years of the electric, lines were rapidly lengthened and service frequently increased. This continuous expansion of surface transportation had a cumulative effect upon the city. The pace of suburbanization, at first slow, went forward with in-

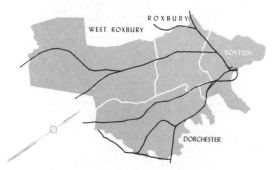

Map 2. Railroad trackage, 1870–1900

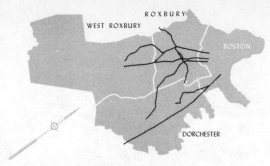

MAP 3. Street railway tracks, 1872

creasing acceleration, until by the 1890's it attained the proportions of a mass movement.

From 1852 until 1873 the horse railroads of Boston merely stretched out the existing city along already established paths. The outer boundary of dense settlement moved perhaps half a mile, so that at the time of the great Depression of 1873 it stood two and a half miles from Boston's City Hall. During the next fourteen years, from 1873 to 1887, horsecar service reached out about a mile and a half farther, bringing the outer edge of good transportation to four miles from City Hall. Lines of suburban settlement began to appear in what were formerly distant places. In the late 1880's and 1890's the electrification of street railways brought convenient transportation to at least the range of six miles from City Hall. The rate of building and settlement in this period became so rapid that the whole scale and plan of Greater Boston was entirely made over.

Boston's first street railway had but one car which in 1852 began service between Harvard Square, Cambridge, and Union Square,

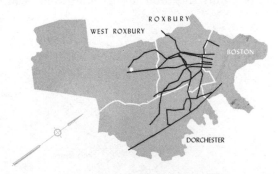

MAP 4. Street railway tracks, 1886

Somerville. The success of this experiment and the example of profitable lines in other American cities brought on a wave of entrepreneurial enthusiasm. To the local investment public, used to the relatively long periods necessary to realize profits on large-scale land speculations, the rapid construction of horse railroads seemed to promise a generous and immediate harvest. To real estate men the simple procedure of placing a coach on iron rails seemed a miraculous device for the promotion of out-of-town property.

The experience of the three towns of Roxbury, West Roxbury, and Dorchester was typical. The first line in this section of the metropolis commenced running in 1856. It followed the seventeenth century path which ran from downtown Boston along Washington street in the South End to Roxbury Crossing. In effect, the new service merely replaced the existing omnibus and supplemented the main traffic of pedestrians and carriages. In the short period from the first incorporation of 1852 to the Depression of 1873, seven companies were formed to serve the outlying towns of Roxbury, West Roxbury, and Dorchester. Only four ever operated. By 1873 only two companies, the Metropolitan Street Railway, and the Highland Street Railway, survived.

Some of Boston's street railways had been projected for routes with too light settlement and traffic, others were badly financed, and some were bogus companies put together to lure investors or to harass operating companies. The scramble for franchises, which were granted by the Boston Board of Aldermen, and for charters of incorporation, which were granted by the state legislature, further confused the ever shifting rivalries of the city's street railway companies.

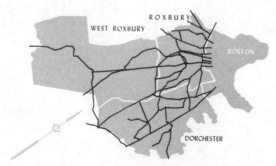

MAP 5. Street railway tracks, 1901

FIG. 8. Horsecar in front of the Metropolitan Street Railway car barn, South and Jamaica streets, Jamaica Plain, West Roxbury, c. 1880

These early difficulties of franchise and capitalization were soon superseded by the problems of the downtown. Boston's streets were just too narrow to carry all the needed cars. The downtown squeeze made necessary complicated lease arrangements for competitors' use

FIG. 9. Open horsecar on Centre street, Jamaica Plain Village, 1883

of each other's tracks. The tempers of street railway employees were not always equal to this requirement of cooperation in a field of intense competition. All too often rival drivers raced for switches, stalled, and in general interfered with each other's progress. Nevertheless, despite early confusion, chicane, and false starts, by 1873 the main streets of the old city had become the new horsecar thoroughfares. During the years from 1852 to 1873 the periphery of dense settlement moved from 2 to 2.5 miles from City Hall.[6]

For the next fourteen years service in Greater Boston expanded steadily outward. Then, in 1887, Henry M. Whitney, a steamship operator and speculator in Brookline real estate, formed a syndicate out of his small West End Street Railway and began to purchase stock in the other five operating companies of Boston. After he had bought up large amounts of stock, especially in the biggest line, the Metropolitan, he offered by an exchange of stock and bonds to combine all the companies into one. Minority stockholders, probably helpless, and at any rate anticipating great profits from the rationalization of Boston service under one giant company, agreed to the merger. At the same time, the promise of rapid expansion of service and relief to downtown traffic jams persuaded the public and the legislature to

Fig. 10. Downtown traffic, Post Office Square, May 23, 1904

allow the creation of the traction monopoly. Consolidation did in fact accelerate the rate of improvements in transportation.

Whitney continued two historic policies of street railway management. First, he was more interested in increasing the total number of fares on his system than in watching the relationship of distance, cost, and fare per ride. He, like his fellow streetcar managers the state over, was so convinced that the key to profit lay in the endless expansion of the numbers of passengers that, with little regard to costs, he constantly expanded the service area of the West End. As a result, by 1900 the outer limits of Boston's electric railways lay at least six miles from the downtown.

Second, Whitney, like all horsecar managers before him, was an ardent believer in the five-cent fare. Thus expansion of service took place without additional charge to the commuter. As crosstown lines were built, free-transfer points were added, so that the nickel fare was almost universal in 1900. During the 1870's and 1880's eight cents had been required for many transfer rides; two full fares had been required where riders moved to the cars of different companies.[7]

In his speeches before city clubs and regulatory agencies Whitney often pointed to these twin policies of rapid service expansion and the uniform five-cent fare as the proper basis for a public transportation system. He was an ardent champion of the suburban city. He frequently appealed to the popular belief that the rapid suburbanization of modern industrial cities was perhaps the most important single contribution of the street railway. Like his listeners, also, Whitney did not wish to control the form and direction of this suburban expansion, but rather to leave the development of suburbs to individual builders and homeowners. Though statistics of 1890 and 1900 showed that only one quarter of Boston's suburbanites owned their houses,[8] he, like his contemporaries, felt that the continued suburbanization of the city would bring a substantial increase in homeownership. He liked to use as a typical example of the coming benefits the rather untypical case of the workingman buying a lot of land in the suburbs upon which would be built his own home. Whitney's speeches were also full of comparisons to conditions in Europe and references to the old pre-streetcar sections of Boston where multifamily tenements and crowded old wooden houses were the rule.

Whitney made these appeals to what was then termed the "moral influence" of street railways both from personal conviction, and from

FIG. 11. Working class wooden houses and tenements in the West End, photograph c. 1890

the need to answer the numerous critics of his monopoly. He was continually before state and city agencies defending the profits and schedules of the West End Street Railway. Most important for the growth of the suburban city, criticism always took for its point of departure the same view of public transportation that Whitney's management undertook to carry out. For critics, the trouble with the West End Company was that its very vigorous performance was not vigorous enough: new service was not added fast enough, profits were too high, and fares not cheap enough.[9]

The demise of Whitney's West End Street Railway as an operating company was due not to the shortcomings of its suburban service, but to continued strife over downtown traffic conditions. The details of the decade of controversy over the control and pricing of tunnels and elevateds are not relevant to this history. In the end, in 1897, a group of rival capitalists formed the Boston Elevated Street Railway Com-

FIG. 12. The moral influence of the street railway, outer edge of new construction, 1904

pany, and, under the supervision of the state-created Boston Transit Authority, leased the West End system in its entirety. With this new operating company the great subway and elevated projects were undertaken in a belated effort to solve downtown traffic problems. The Boston Elevated's suburban policy remained that of its predecessors: expand for more total passengers.

During the entire second half of the nineteenth century two things made possible this continuous expansion of service under all kinds of managements. The first was the declining costs of materials; the second was electrification. In 1888 the West End began experimenting with electric cars and in 1889 introduced its first trolley service. The electric car moved at least twice as fast as the horse drawn one and soon was perfected to carry three times the number of passengers. Of course offsetting these advantages, the new machines required a great deal more investment in heavy equipment than the horse and his carbarn.

In the center of the system, where traffic was heavy, the electric car was cheaper to operate per passenger mile than the horsecar. It seemed reasonable to run the electric car from the intown segment of a line out to the suburban terminal, especially since in the outer areas of less frequent stops the electric could really show its speed. In this way the electric-powered streetcar beguiled traction men who were careless about costs into spinning out the web of their service even beyond profitable limits.[10]

OTHER SERVICES TO HOME BUILDERS

Good transportation was not the only requirement for the successful large-scale development of suburban land, nor was the street railway the only important invention which contributed to the changing pattern of Greater Boston. During the last third of the nineteenth century sanitation and power services became established as prerequisites for the standard home.

Until the 1870's the cities and towns of the metropolitan region had relied upon a mixture of public and private agencies for water supply and waste disposal. Municipal and private scavengers carried off rubbish, garbage, and privy waste. Some crowded districts had cooperative underground sewer lines, others did not. Because the discharge points were unregulated by anything but the common law of nuisance many of the low lands and neighborhood swamps of the

FIG. 13. Typical electric streetcar, 1900

Fig. 14. Open electric car for summer service, about 1903

region were terminal sewage pools. In crowded town centers, where surface wells proved inadequate, public and private water companies had been formed to meet group needs. The City of Boston's Cochituate Water Works of the 1840's was the most famous and largest of the systems. All the municipal and private systems together, however, failed to give more than partial coverage to the metropolis.

Partial coverage was almost useless to a public health program. The periodic plagues and epidemics that had swept the city regularly since the seventeenth century gave frequent demonstration that no part of the metropolis was safe until all parts were clean. By 1870 Boston's own efforts and other American and European sanitary projects showed that the incidence of disease could be effectively reduced by thoroughgoing sanitary engineering. Fear of disease gave the late nineteenth century public health movement its great popularity, while the concurrent benefits of water for industrial use and fire protection assisted reformers in arguments with cost-conscious taxpayers.

During the last third of the nineteenth century Boston's sanitary projects, its waterworks, sewer lines, land filling, and regrading took about one third of the total city budget. Homeowners installed their own plumbing, and water meters and special installation assessments paid for the operating costs. But the enormous initial expenditure demanded for water mains, reservoirs, pumping stations, and trunk sewers could only have been met by the pledge of municipal and state credit.[11]

Historically public interest in the supply of water preceded interest in waste disposal. Consequently the water and sewer systems of the metropolis continued under separate institutional management throughout the century. The great popularity of the sanitary engineering program assured strong public support, first for town and city boards, and later for the integrating metropolitan boards. As a result of the public enthusiasm, expenditures were usually generous and the planning of the works aggressive. As fast as new street railway transportation brought new houses to outlying parts of the city the sanitary departments hastened to provide facilities.[12]

The lesser utilities—gas, electricity, and telephones—were developed by private corporations. The convenience of gas and electric lights, and the efficiency of telephone communication gave private companies marketable products for which users would pay the whole cost. Also, because these minor utilities did not need to cover the whole city at once they could seek the highest paying users first, and then expand their systems on a profit making basis. The extension of gas service, which began in the 1840's, and the extension of electric and telephone services, which began in the 1890's, were clearly derivative. Once street railways and sanitary engineering opened an area to home building the other utilities sought customers there. Most of the utility conflicts of the day concerned consumer rates, not the slowness of new service offerings.[13]

COMMON PATTERNS OF DECISION

Because of the aggressive quality of the public health movement and the imitative nature of the lesser utilities and municipal services the narrative of the development of the Boston metropolis during the last third of the nineteenth century can be simplified. Had these utilities and municipal services lagged significantly behind transportation, or had they pursued a radically different timing and pattern of location they would require an extensive separate treatment. As it was, the role of the large public and private institutions in the building of the metropolis can be analyzed in terms of the street railway alone.

It is important to notice that certain ideas were common to all institutional decision makers of the last third of the nineteenth century.

First, within their financial means all institutions undertook to render equal service throughout their geographic jurisdiction. Second, none of the institutions built houses themselves and, as much as possible, they avoided interfering with private profit making. Indeed, all encouraged individual capitalist enterprise as much as they could. Third, all institutions were somewhat sympathetic to the goals of the rural ideal, and to the extent that their actions were relevant, encouraged the dispersal of the urban population.

Although Boston society suffered severe ethnic tensions during this period of large scale immigration, its public agencies pursued a policy of service without regard to ethnic background. Just as the streetcar companies undertook to serve all the villages and quarters of the metropolitan region, so the schools and libraries undertook to serve all the children and adults within the municipality. Sewer, water, gas, and electric utilities were available at uniform prices to users everywhere.[14] Water was as plentiful in the immigrant North End as in the native Back Bay.

If there were unsanitary conditions in the slums, such conditions were regarded as the responsibility of landlords and tenants. The evidence of disease-ridden slums in an era of great concern for public health illustrates the second policy of public agencies in the late nineteenth century. Effective devices were developed for bringing public services to the property owner. The supervision of property owners' individual performances, however, was lightly touched upon, and no effective machinery was devised for public assumption of responsibility when the owners failed in their performance.[15] The official policy was to interfere as little as possible with individuals, and, where possible, to assist individuals in their role as private capitalists.

The contrast between the achievements in the old slum neighborhoods and the new suburbs graphically demonstrates the results of this policy. In the slums agencies dealt with individuals whose means were inadequate to the task; in the suburbs the public effort met immediate and effective private response. In the suburbs water lines, sewers, and public utilities hurried along with new construction, while the public transportation was extended with uniform fares to ever greater distances from the city. Likewise, at enormous cost, schools, libraries, fire stations, indeed, all municipal services, hastened after the movement of people within the metropolis.[16]

The City of Boston, the Metropolitan Commissioners, the West End Street Railway, and the predecessors of the Boston Consolidated Gas and Boston Edison companies all extended their services at a very rapid rate. They were able to do so because their fees and taxes rested upon large and prosperous geographical bases. Where the geographical units were small and poor, as was the case in most of the towns beyond five miles from Boston, the rate of progress was slow. The water pipes rarely ran beyond Main Street, and community expansion consisted of the building of a graded primary school, or, perhaps, the addition of those two new municipal ornaments, the high school and the public library.

Today's municipal planning policy rests on a conscious attempt to control the uses of land. One of the major goals of modern planning is to allocate the various uses of land with an end to minimizing public costs and maximizing public benefits. Though in today's terms there was no planning in late nineteenth century Boston, the largely successful effort to give new services to the whole jurisdiction with its consequent aid to private development was a conscious policy designed to achieve the ends of society. By providing equal service to all citizens, by extending service as rapidly as possible to the whole geographic jurisdiction, Boston's public agencies hoped to give the greatest scope to the workings of individual capitalists. Education, health, transportation, and plentiful land were tools to encourage individuals to work effectively as private profit makers. The works of the individual private profit makers were to be the return for the public costs and effort.[17]

The third policy of the public agencies was to encourage the dispersal of the urban population. Tenement slums were the scandal of the age. Street railway managers, real estate men, politicians, philanthropists, health officers, school teachers, and the middle class generally all shared the attitude that open country surroundings and the small community were beneficent settings for family life. This widespread sympathy for the rural ideal provided additional impetus for the expansion of public services over the entire metropolitan region.[18]

The most general result of the work of the large institutions of Greater Boston was to make possible the creation of a new environment in the suburban edge of the metropolis while, at the same time, leaving the intown section largely undisturbed. Much of this onesided effect upon the physical plan of the metropolis must be attributed to the continued need of close proximity for daily work.

Though railroads and steamships brought goods and passengers from great distances with unprecedented speed, though the street rail-

way daily moved thousands of commuters, though telephones, tele-
graphs, and railway mail connected all sections of the metropolis to
the nation, much of the economic life of 1900 still depended upon
physical proximity. As only some customers and suppliers had telephones, office boys bearing notes were still a major form of rapid
communication; hand carts and wagons and teams were still the
methods of moving small lots of goods from ship to warehouse, from
freight car to factory and shop, from store to customer. Because
of these limited means of communication the work and shopping center of Boston remained packed tight against the harbor. Larger
wharves, warehouses, and railway yards were built at or near old locations; offices, stores, and factories replaced houses. And in the downtown core tall buildings with elevators replaced the former five-story
walk-ups.

The novel contribution of the street railway came in the zone beyond the old central city where the new transportation allowed the
wide diffusion of the residential area. Most of the extension of the
metropolis that took place with the establishment of street railways
benefited middle-income families. Though they still had to seek their
livelihood in the central city, their homes spread over an unprecedented
area of suburban land. During the last fifty years of the nineteenth
century Greater Boston tripled its population, but the houses of the
new suburbs generally had two and often three times the land of their
predecessors, and such was the revolution in transportation that even
after such rapid growth vast amounts of vacant land still remained
for future building.[19]

To see the full effects of the policy and work of the large institutions
upon the construction of the new suburbs one must look at the patterns of building in some detail. Since the final decision of whether or
not to put up a house rested with thousands of individual landowners,
one must look closely at a small area, an area which reflects the scale
of their decisions. Three Boston streetcar suburbs, the former towns of
Roxbury, West Roxbury, and Dorchester, will serve as the area
of detailed study. During the last third of the nineteenth century
these towns experienced an enormous growth of population, and over
much of their territory the pattern of streets and houses took on the
new suburban form. Even today the achievements and shortcomings
of this former era continue to dominate their life.

CHAPTER THREE

THE THREE TOWNS

THE THREE formerly independent towns of Roxbury, West Roxbury, and Dorchester together provide an ideal example of streetcar suburbs. By the scale of the old pedestrian city of 1850 they were enormous. The area was composed primarily of residences, and the arrangement of the houses was such that today the towns appear both repetitious and confusing. Their experience during the last third of the nineteenth century was typical of what took place in all the cities and towns around Boston, and probably of what took place in similar areas throughout the country.

Sheer size was an important characteristic of the towns. Although in 1900 their territory constituted only the southern segment of metropolitan Boston, their expanse of twenty-five and a quarter square miles more than doubled the area of the whole 1850 pre-streetcar metropolis.[1] Most of this land lay beyond the zone of dense settlement of the days of the walking city. In 1870, after the first fifteen years of the horsecar and the tentative beginnings of suburbanization, the towns held a population of 60,000; in 1900 they had boomed to 227,000. This thirty-year growth was of the same order of magnitude as that which took place within the city limits of San Francisco; and had the combined population of the towns been counted as a unit it would have ranked with cities like Washington, Newark, and Louisville.[2] The amount of new residential construction was substantial. In thirty years 22,500 houses went up: 12,000 single-family houses, 6,000 two-family houses, 4,000 three-family houses, and about 500 larger structures. Altogether, these provided homes for 167,000 new suburbanites.

The confusing appearance of these old suburbs adds to their

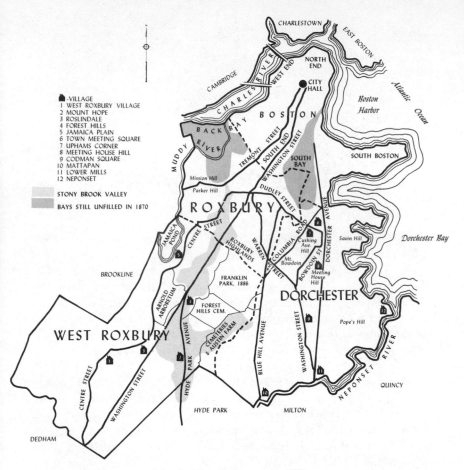

MAP 6. The three towns in 1870

typicality. Twentieth century observers have coined the term "suburban sprawl" to describe the modern residential growth of American cities. This term of criticism implies a lack of order, a seeming incomprehensibility in the physical arrangements of suburbs. Its aptness comes from two conditions. The shape of the land is buried under endless streets, streets so filled with houses and so patched together that the observer cannot orient himself in a landscape larger than a block or two. Second, in old suburbs the successive construction of various styles and types of buildings has so jumbled together houses of successive periods that today it requires careful study to reconstruct the organization of each era.

The present disorder of the streetcar suburbs is a direct product of the manner in which they were built, but nothing could be further from the truth than to say they were the product of disorganization. The three towns of Roxbury, West Roxbury, and Dorchester were built by a strict discipline, a discipline of nineteeth century conditions which organized the structures and their builders into patterns which, in their way, were as rigid as any modern development statutes.

THE DISCIPLINE OF HISTORY AND GEOGRAPHY

The 22,500 new dwellings of Roxbury, West Roxbury, and Dorchester were the product of separate decisions made by 9,000 individual builders. Some of these builders were carpenters, some real estate men, but most were not professionals at all. The vast majority were either men building houses for their own occupancy or small investors who built a house nearby their own residence in order to profit from the rents of one to three tenants. For the purposes of this book the "builders" are all these decision makers of whatever occupation, the men and women who owned the land upon which a house was to be built. The City of Boston's Building Permits listed these decision makers by name as the owners of the land at the time the permit was issued. These were the people who, at the very least, had to give their consent before any new construction could take place. They and the large utilities and municipal institutions together built the new suburbs.

No legislation save the law of nuisance and a few primitive safety codes prevented these 9,000 landowners from doing anything they wanted with their property. Nevertheless, they were not really free agents. Nor did the franchise of the street railway or the statutory authority of the water board make these free agents. All the decision makers, whether small owners or large institutions, depended upon the inherited conditions of the property they worked upon. The street railway company had to view what existed with an eye to traffic potential, grades, and ease of connection with existing carlines; the water board worked with analogous considerations. In these calculations the inheritance of the past entered into the day's decisions.

An individual builder contemplating the purchase of a house lot, or deciding what kind of a house to put up, concerned himself with a whole set of pre-existing and expected conditions. There were the obvious economic concerns. Was the price of the land more than he could afford? Was the transportation adequate? Were municipal water and sewer lines handy? Was there gas nearby? Was the neighborhood prosperous and growing? Would the house rent well and sell easily? What sort of tenants and purchasers could be expected? The concern for the occupancy of the contemplated structure led to other questions. What kind of people lived nearby? Who was moving into the area? Were there satisfactory schools and parks?

Few, perhaps, made a mental check list of questions and then ticked them off, but all these questions were subsumed under two questions which every decision maker must have asked himself: Can I afford it? Do I want to live here? These twin questions permeated every builder's actions, whether the builder was putting up his first and only house or was a speculator. It was through this analysis of the situation that the force of history and geography came to discipline the actions of the 9,000 separate decision makers and the large institutions.

The three former towns of Roxbury, West Roxbury, and Dorchester constituted a single segment of the metropolitan Boston transportation system. They did so because of their geography. In 1870 the South and Back bays had only been partially filled. Between the two bays the narrow South End of Boston connected Roxbury with the city proper. This constriction forced all the transportation lines from Boston to assume a radial pattern. The roads and later streetcar lines all crowded together along the South End and then opened out in Roxbury and fanned over the distant suburbs. The eastern and western boundaries of the three-town district were sharply defined. To the east the Atlantic Ocean bounded one side of Dorchester; to the West the swamps and marshes of the Jamaica Pond, Muddy River, and Back Bay set a substantial boundary to Roxbury and inner West Roxbury. With the exception of Tremont street in Roxbury, which led west to Brookline, and Dorchester avenue, which skitted across a narrow strip of land on the eastern shore to South Boston, none of the major arteries of the towns served another peripheral Boston community.

Beyond the South End constriction the rough contours of the land did much to bend and twist the paths of transportation. Despite successive changes in land uses and transportation methods the contours of the land continued to shape the growth of the towns. Washington street, Roxbury,* and its branches of Centre street and Hyde Park avenue led to the outer villages of Jamaica Plain, West Roxbury, and Hyde Park. This branching of roads described at once the main valleys of the uplands of West Roxbury, the principal north-south traffic movement, the location of most of the eighteenth and nineteenth century farms and villages, the streetcar lines, the railroad route, and the main lines of suburban development.

The other main traffic axes of the towns had much the same characteristics. The network that joined Roxbury and Dorchester skirted the hills of Roxbury highlands and then followed the ridges of land in the Dorchester uplands. Warren street in Roxbury and Blue Hill avenue, Washington street, and Bowdoin street in Dorchester formed a basic north-south transportation system. These roads were both the simplest way to connect up the sloping farm lands of Dorchester and (later) the cheapest way to reach the houses built on those farms. Another main artery, Dorchester avenue, was a simple north-south sea-level route that followed the shore and was later imitated by the railroad, streetcar lines, and finally two superhighways. The other important traffic artery of the towns was Dudley street in Roxbury and Dorchester. It was an east-west road which ran from Roxbury Crossing, through the center of lower Roxbury to Upham's Corner, an old intown center of Dorchester. This road followed the fifty-foot contour line, where the steep grades of the upland met the level plain and marsh of the South Bay. Although the significance of these main paths is now obscured by the numerous grids of streets which have been joined to them, their influence upon the basic flow of traffic and upon the pattern of building was decisive. In the simplest terms, both farmers and suburbanites began first where the land was handy and then worked out to the back lots and the high stony plots.

In 1870 Roxbury was by far the most densely settled of the three

* Excluding the Washington avenues, alleys, and boulevards, there are at the moment of writing thirty-six Washington streets in metropolitan Boston, six in the different quarters of Boston itself. For the purposes of this book the reader should distinguish between two different Washington streets. One is the long street which runs north and south from the downtown shopping center of the city, along the South End, through Roxbury, up the Stony Brook Valley to Forest Hills, West Roxbury, and thence through West Roxbury until it passes out of the city limits into Dedham. The other important Washington street is in Dorchester. This street, which is unconnected to its Roxbury counterpart, begins at Blue Hill avenue and runs through Codman Square to the village of Lower Mills, where it ends in a junction with Dorchester avenue.

towns. Its geography divided the town's settlement into two parts: the highlands, the steep uplands south of Dudley street; and lower Roxbury, the intown lowlands that stretch from the South End to Dudley street. Despite a marked separation in the land uses of the two districts—the highlands being largely residential; lower Roxbury, a mixed industrial and residential area—a number of characteristics showed that the Roxbury of 1870 was as yet not a modern suburb. The modern suburb's segregation of residence and business and the segregation of residences by classes had not yet taken place. Until the Depression of 1873 there was a continued building of city row houses, the invasion of the highlands by a large factory, and the juxtaposition of many classes in lower Roxbury.

Roxbury in 1870 was developing from the patterns of the old peripheral towns of the earlier era of the walking city. In the twenty years from 1850 to 1870 Roxbury had enjoyed a great industrial and building boom, but much of today's lower Roxbury was at this time still the unfilled marshes and flats of the Back and South bays. Along the edge of these marshes lived the poor of Roxbury, the shanty Irish, drawn there by the cheapness of the land and the nearness to Roxbury manufacturing plants, and by the fact that it was within walking distance of work in Boston.

The rest of the lowlands was shared by a variety of users. The largest industrial concentration of the whole three-town area grew up here, supported by the water and power from the Stony Brook and Back Bay, and by the docking facilities of the South Bay. Foundries, textile mills, rope walks, piano works, clock companies, lumber and stone yards, indeed, all sorts of establishments, appeared between Dudley street and the Boston line. In effect, the inner section of Roxbury was a continuation of the South End–South Boston industrial complex. During the years 1830–1860 large numbers of mill workers' row houses were constructed near the factories; by 1870 this was the working class area, even the pauper and slum section, of the three towns. These were not the packed slums of Boston's North End or New York City, but rather a small drab section of little two- and three-story wooden houses and barracks such as could be found in any New England mill town.

The lowness of most of the land of inner Roxbury made the whole area subject to periodic flooding by storm tides of the Atlantic and, less frequently, by floods of the Stony Brook.* These same conditions made the construction of adequate sewers expensive. Though by 1870 Roxbury was an industrial city of 23,000 the city fathers had done little to solve this problem. Ironically, the greatest municipal venture up to the annexation of Roxbury to Boston was the construction of the beautiful Forest Hills Cemetery in what became West Roxbury. The persistent need for expensive public works was one important factor behind the many citizens' petitions for annexation to Boston. In 1868 the city of Roxbury voted to join Boston, and although it took them more than twenty years, Boston engineers finally brought the Stony Brook under control and established adequate sanitary facilities in lower Roxbury.

The steep hills of outer Roxbury, that part of the town south of Dudley street, had an entirely different character. Here in 1870 were the substantial middle class houses of Boston businessmen and the handsome estates of an earlier era. Since the beginning of the century this had been a popular area for country seats. After the 1840's the railroad, the omnibus, and finally the horsecar brought to this section hundreds of middle class Bostonians, families following the fashion set by their wealthy predecessors. In this sense Roxbury highlands shared a partial suburbanization with the nonfarming part of West Roxbury.

In general West Roxbury was a rough and wooded district except for three tracts of comparatively level ground. The most famous of these was Jamaica Plain which since the eighteenth century had been a fashionable summering place for the rich. Governor Francis Bernard and John Hancock made their homes there. The reason was simple enough: Jamaica Plain was the first scenic piece of high ground one reached on the only road from Boston.

During the 1820's a charming rural village grew up near Jamaica Pond and along the main street of the town, Centre street, which was formerly the highway to Dedham. This cluster was to become the political and social center of West Roxbury. With the coming of the railroad in 1835 active speculation in house lots for businessmen sprang

---

* The once troublesome Stony Brook is now totally encased in a culvert which runs parallel to Washington street in West Roxbury and joins the Muddy River in the Back Bay Fens Park. This park was built in the shape of a large bowl so that in times of storms it could act as a flood storage basin.

up, and by 1870 a substantial suburban colony like those of inner Dorchester and Roxbury highlands had developed in Jamaica Plain. Despite such changes the center of West Roxbury endeavored to preserve its former rural character against the coming of modern municipal life. In 1851 it separated itself from its parent city of Roxbury in a last attempt to continue as a country town. By 1873 the real estate promoters and commuters so predominated that they carried the town into union with Boston.

Even in the 1870's a series of small villages lay amidst the farm land that stretched out along Centre and Washington streets south of Jamaica Plain. The largest plateau of open land made up Roslindale and West Roxbury villages, one and three miles distant from Jamaica Plain, respectively. Another fairly level area, the valley of Stony Brook, stretched in one continuous line from Roxbury Crossing to Forest Hills and Mt. Hope. This was the valley that the main line of the railroad followed. The farthest of the villages, Mt. Hope, consisted of a few farms, but much of the rest of the valley was becoming industrialized. From Roxbury Crossing to Forest Hills stood a series of mills and shops. Most notable were the tanneries and breweries. A few of the latter remain to this day. This manufacturing district separated the two upper middle class residential settlements of Jamaica Plain and Roxbury highlands. Near the factories were strings of German and Irish workers' houses. In 1870 these workers were a convenient source of domestic help; by 1900 they were heirs apparent to the whole district.

The geography of Dorchester also exerted a strong influence upon its development. The unfilled South Bay isolated the town from Boston, although the inner portions of Dorchester lay but two miles from the center of the city. Dorchester's lack of water power except at the distant Neponset River, which was at the southernmost end of town, five miles from Boston, prevented any continuous band of industrial development like the Stony Brook of Roxbury and West Roxbury.

From a high ridge which ran approximately along Washington street the land of the town sloped off eastward to the sea, its more or less gentle slopes interrupted here and there by five hills: Mt. Bowdoin, Pope's Hill, Meeting House Hill, Cushing Avenue Hill, and Savin Hill. Thus, Dorchester contained two quite even areas, a high plateau to the south and west of the Washington street ridge, and an eastern slope that stretched down to the water. These large and even areas were ideally suited to inexpensive residential construction, but in 1870 they were too far for mass commuting to Boston and most of their surface was taken up by truck gardens and other small farms.

During the years 1850–1870 inner Dorchester—the villages of Upham's Corner, Town Meeting Square, and Meeting House Hill—experienced a small suburban boom. By 1870 its main streets and some rear blocks were peppered with commuters' houses.

THE THREE TOWNS, 1870–1900

The suburbanization of the three towns of Roxbury, West Roxbury, and Dorchester came on in two waves. The first beginning wave was the postwar boom that lasted from 1865 to 1873. During these years the tentative patterns of the development of middle class commuting suburbs can be discovered in Roxbury highlands, Jamaica Plain, and inner Dorchester. The Depression of 1873 slowed construction for a time and then in the mid-1880's and the 1890's a second and gigantic boom began. Roxbury was completely covered with houses, Dorchester and West Roxbury were about half filled.

The results of the building boom of the 1880's and 1890's differed substantially from what had gone before. The overwhelming amount of construction was residential. No growth of industry attracted the towns' new residents. They were commuters whose jobs remained in the old sections of Boston. The amount of land allocated to each house was unprecedented. Even cheap multiple dwellings had lots as generous as those of contemporary expensive Back Bay construction. The average suburban house enjoyed at least twice the yard of intown styles. The architecture was also novel. The detached wooden house, especially the single-family house, predominated. An enormous public effort accompanied this house building. Dozens of schools, libraries, and minor public buildings were put up. The major part of Boston's park system—including Franklin Park, Franklin Field, the Arboretum, and the Jamaica Pond–Muddy River system—was purchased and constructed during the last third of the century. The result of this total building effort was to create in the three towns a pervading sense of newness.

In 1899, a longtime resident of Dorchester, Reverend Samuel J. Barrows, reviewed the recent history of his town. He noted two essential changes: the town was both new and big. Everywhere the new obscured

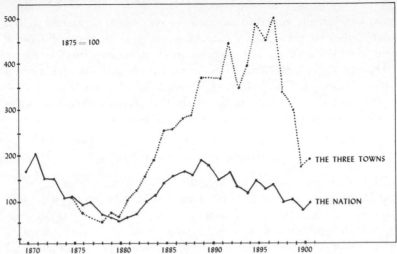

1875 = 100

THE THREE TOWNS

THE NATION

NEW RESIDENTIAL CONSTRUCTION, 1870–1901, the three towns and the nation. The index for the three towns was constructed from a count of the building permits issued by the City of Boston from the first full year in which all the towns were annexed. The national index was adapted from Clarence D. Long, *Building Cycles and the Theory of Investment* (Princeton, 1940), Appendix B, section 3.

the old, and such was the extent of new things and new people that he despaired of ever knowing his fellow citizens or comprehending his new environment. To him the former village life was lost.[3]

Novel though they were, the suburbs were a curious blend of old conditions and old ways with new ideas and new engineering. The old transportation paths of the eighteenth and early nineteenth centuries, set as they were by the topography of the land, continued to influence the development of the three towns and to discipline the movements of the new suburbanites. The new engineering of boulevards and street railways was used mainly to enlarge existing paths. No attempt was made, excepting perhaps the widening of Columbia road in Dorchester, to deal with the traffic problems presented by the growth of the village and mill clusters of 60,000 inhabitants into a densely settled suburb of 227,000.

The same historical patterns of villages, farm roads, and fields also determined most of the layout of the minor streets. Developers purchased small tracts as they were offered and fitted new streets and houses to the established lines. As a result, not only were the major traffic movements to and from Boston inherited from the past but the circulation within the neighborhoods was permanently set by the past. Just as the existing industrial concentrations and cheap housing tended to attract more of the same, so the reputation of existing villages, the fashionable tone of Jamaica Plain, Roxbury highlands, or Savin Hill, tended to attract families of similar income and aspiration.

Finally, the presence of farms and open land both at the outer edge of settlement and in undeveloped pockets all through the three towns obscured from the suburbanites the true nature of their environment. As Reverend Barrows observed, they were building a wholly new environment, but the omnipresence of vacant land lulled builders into having no thought of the future. Each homeowner wanted to believe that his new house was in the country, or at least near it, though in fact in ten to fifteen years his house and land would be lost in a great plain of new streets and new houses.

CHAPTER FOUR

A SELECTIVE MELTING POT

DURING THE years 1870–1900 one basic pattern organized the whole suburban metropolis: people were separated by income and mixed together with little regard to national origin. Although ethnic concentrations continually appeared, such groupings were strictly temporary and subsidiary clusters subject to the general movement of people by income capability and income identification. Indeed an observation of the timing and the degree of concentration of these clusters provides the historian with a good measure of the democratic openness of Boston society.

The overall metropolitan pattern of residences was achieved in three ways: by the division of the city into those who could afford new and recent construction and those who could not; by the division of the middle and upper classes according to their varying transportation needs; and by the force of historic conditions within small geographic areas upon the decisions of the individual builders. The first two can be observed by an examination of the relationship of the pattern of class segregation to the expansion of street railways within the area of the three towns. The force of historic conditions will then be taken up in an examination of three smaller cases: central Dorchester, lower Roxbury, and Roxbury highlands.

Throughout the last third of the nineteenth century the old walking city was predominantly the region of cheap secondhand housing. The outer edge of this region lay at a distance of 2 to 2.5 miles from Boston's City Hall. Beyond was the land of new suburban construction. This crude division of the metropolis into two parts manifested itself in several ways. The boundary between the two parts separated the inner area of concentrated working class settlement from the outer area of middle class predominance; the land of the new immigrant from the land of the second generation and assimilated Americans. It was a highly visible boundary, a boundary between tenements and row houses on the one hand and the new detached wooden houses of the streetcar era on the other.

In metropolitan Boston from 1870 to 1900, if a house was new it was suburban. There were but two major exceptions to this rule: the new Back Bay row houses and the new workers' tenements. Both were special forms of the central city. Long after the row house had been abandoned elsewhere in Greater Boston, the Back Bay continued its special architecture. This area was able to develop as a handsome anachronism because it was isolated from the main nineteenth century commercial traffic of the metropolis, and because the state regulated its land use and construction practices.

Special conditions also fostered tenement construction. In this case building depended upon the continued and extensive immigration of

Fig. 15. Speculator's 1887 Back Bay row houses, 517–523 Beacon street

cheap labor into the work center of the city. Here, in the crowded blocks of the North, South, and West ends, close to jobs and close to fellow immigrants, new life in America began. New tenements, like conversions of old houses, provided a financially possible system of housing for Boston's low-rent population because they allotted very little space to each person. Not only were the rooms small but several families often shared single apartments, or families would take in boarders.

Outside the old walking city the metropolitan population was further divided. In the suburbs segregation resulted from the varying income capabilities and transportation needs of the different segments of the middle and upper classes. This segregation was a complicated

Fig. 16. Dense West End land plan, code tenements c. 1890. Buildings now torn down

process which depended upon the interaction of the arrival of various kinds of transportation service with the timing of the building booms.

In one elemental way street railway service and suburban house building moved together: the more street railway service, the faster the rate of building. The early lines of the 1870's which ran through the fields and farms to the small villages 3 and 5 miles from downtown Boston were clearly in advance of active building. The first service on these distant lines offered only one car every hour. Later as traffic increased more cars were assigned to the run. Like the railroads these first tracks fanned out from the center of the city and lacked any suburban interconnections. Nevertheless, the more frequent stops of the streetcar gave its service a special quality. As opposed to the quarter-mile intervals between the railroad stations the streetcar provided an unbroken line of service from its suburban terminal to the downtown. In this way each line opened for building a continuous strip of land instead of isolated areas around each station. Indeed, until electrics were introduced in 1889, suburban horsecars slowed down for passengers anywhere along their route, coming to a full stop only for ladies.

In metropolitan Boston the street railway always offered three kinds of service and each kind of service attracted a particular pattern of residential building. Pioneering lines with infrequent service to outlying areas when first instituted merely supplemented the steam railroad's commuter service. After some years, however, homes would appear, not as formerly, clustered about the station villages, but in lines parallel to the streetcar tracks.

Next came the institution of good linear service, a car about every ten minutes. This increase in service generally brought a jump in the rate of building, but the pattern of building remained restricted to following the streetcar lines. The effect of the pioneering service and the good linear service was the same, but they may be usefully distinguished by the frequency of cars and the rate of building. For example, in 1872 a line ran out Washington street from Boston, through the South End to Roxbury, and thence out Centre street to Jamaica Plain. The Boston to Roxbury segment of the line gave good linear service, cars every eight minutes; the Roxbury to Jamaica Plain segment was a pioneering one: it had cars only every half hour. There was a marked difference in the rates of building next to the two segments, building along the Roxbury to Boston segment being far the most active.

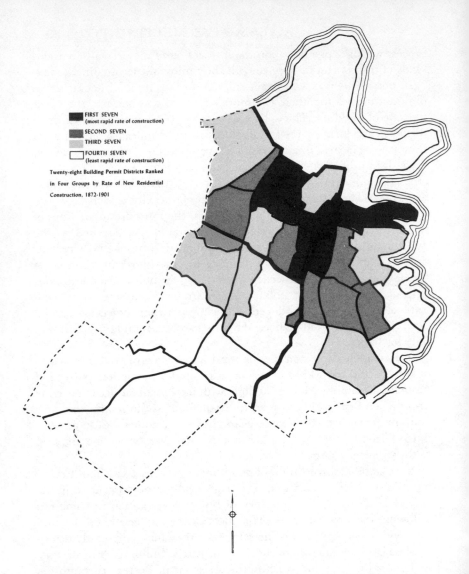

MAP 7. Rate of new residential construction, three towns, 1872–1901. This map is a condensation of a house-by-house plotting of all new residential construction in the three towns. The source was the building permits for the years 1872–1901. The towns were divided into twenty-eight districts, shown in outline here. For a full series of maps giving house-by-house locations, further discussion of method, and statistical tables of dwelling location and its relation to street railway service, train service, population, school building, and churches see Warner, "Residential Development," Appendix E and Atlas.

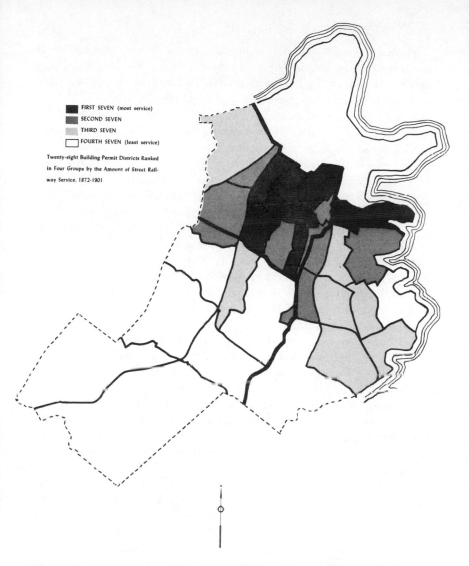

Map legend:
FIRST SEVEN (most service)
SECOND SEVEN
THIRD SEVEN
FOURTH SEVEN (least service)

Twenty-eight Building Permit Districts Ranked
in Four Groups by the Amount of Street Railway Service, 1872-1901

MAP 8. Amount of street railway service in the three towns, 1872–1901. The street railway service was assumed to be that advertised by the companies in the Boston Street Directory and listed in "Boston Elevated and West End Street Railway, Historical Dates Since January 2, 1892" (MS, Boston Elevated Railway Library, Metropolitan Transit Authority, Boston, Mass.). Each building permit district was rated on the basis of the amount of service per hour at one theoretical point within its boundaries. All service on lines within and tangent to the boundaries of a district was counted as contributing to the service at the one theoretical point.

From 1870 to 1900 the outer limits of street railway service moved ever farther from Boston as new tracks were laid, but the relationship of the outer lines to building was always the same: it was linear service and encouraged building in parallel lines of development.

Finally, as land adjacent to these lines of linear service filled up with houses to a width of easy walking distance on each side, more service became necessary, both along the original route and along new routes which would connect these strips of new houses. Crosstown lines and complementary connections of villages lying at the same general distance from the city became profitable. At the time when crosstown service began to be established the extension of streetcar service ceased to be a predominant cause of house building. Now the building began to encourage the expansion of service as well as the service encouraging building. As time went on and this process continued, new tracks were laid ever farther from the center of the city, first in the linear pattern, then in the crosstown pattern.

By 1900, with the elevated and rapid transit still to be built, the outer limits of convenient street railway commuting stood about 6 miles from City Hall. By transferring one could travel 10 miles and even farther, but good linear service, with cars at ten- to fifteen-minute intervals, extended only 6 miles out. In 1900 a 6-mile trip, with a short walk to the car and the frequent stops of an ordinary surface ride, meant an hour's time from home to office. Beyond the 6-mile limit commuters depended upon the faster and more expensive railroad service. The number of people able to afford railroad transportation, however, was limited to a small prosperous segment of the population.

In terms of urban building the result of the 1870–1900 expansion of the street railway was to open up to the great mass of Boston's middle class that enormous expanse of land beyond the harbor which lay in the previously lightly settled zone of 2.5 to 6 miles from the downtown. The upper half of Boston's population enjoyed in the last third of the nineteenth century roughly a sixfold increase in its area of settlement.

The Street Railway and Class Building Patterns

Now the opening up of this great tract of land did not come all in one year. The pace of building was not steady; there were boom years and idle years. Moreover, owners of land did not offer their fields and estates all at once; some tracts were quickly sold to speculators; others remained in one family for long periods. These variations had by 1900 made some of the neighborhoods of Roxbury, West Roxbury, and Dorchester composites of the building patterns of the various segments of the middle class. Other neighborhoods had a design and character which reflected occupancy by only one segment of the middle class. To understand the relationship between transportation and building and the segregation which resulted it is useful to consider the suburban building process as if income and transportation were the two factors which affected the location of new houses. Many other factors combined to form the character of new neighborhoods: churches, home finance, and the like. These will be added to the story later.

The upper-income half of Greater Boston's population of the period from 1870 to 1900 may be divided into three categories: the wealthy, constituting 5 percent of the whole population; the central middle class, 15 percent; the lower middle class, 20 to 30 percent.

The first category included the richest 1 percent of the population, what in the nineteenth century might have been called "gentlemen of wealth and leisure," and the upper middle class: large storeowners, successful manufacturers, brokers, wholesalers, and prosperous lawyers. In terms of housing, their tastes advertised the fashions of the day and their habits presented models for the rest of the middle class. The richest among them sometimes purchased an expensive town house in the Back Bay, sometimes built estates in the country, sometimes even owned both. Many, however, took advantage of their greater control over hours of work and the fashion for suburban life to build big houses on the best streets and finest prospects of suburban Boston. Such houses appeared both at great distance from Boston where railroad transportation had to be relied upon, and closer to town in the old high-priced pockets of land where former estates had been cut up into large and expensive parcels. Sections of Jamaica Plain and Roxbury highlands throughout the last third of the nineteenth century enjoyed a steady building up of such enclaves. Dorchester and most suburban communities came to contain at least a few streets and houses of Boston's wealthy.

The central middle class—the owners of small downtown stores, successful salesmen and commercial travelers, lawyers, school teachers,

Fig. 17. Upper middle class suburban street, c. 1890

Fig. 18. Pre-suburban housing of the central middle class, c. 1850

and the large contractors—constituted about 15 percent of Boston's population during this period. This is the group that common opinion has rightly associated with the suburbs. They had stricter transportation needs. Their hours of work were long, but unlike the lower middle class their places of work tended to be stable so that they had a predictable route of travel. Nor was multiple employment a necessity for these families. As a result good linear streetcar service, or even railroad service if the stations were handy, was all they required.

Prior to the horsecar such families had lived in brick row houses in the West End, in the new South End, and along the former residential streets to the south and east of the Boston Common. Others of the group had sought inexpensive land in Charlestown, Cambridge, Roxbury, and South and East Boston from whence they commuted by omnibus or on foot. With the pressure of commercial expansion and immigrant workers on their old neighborhoods, and the simultaneous opportunity for suburban living, they moved in large numbers out of the old city and along the new horsecar lines. With the establishment in the period 1870–1900 of good linear service 2.5 to 6 miles

FIG. 19. Suburban house of the central middle class, c. 1885

from downtown Boston came the construction of acres of suburban single- and two-family houses, houses that fulfilled many of the needs and desires of this central segment of Boston's middle class.[1]

The largest segment of Boston's population that could purchase new homes required good transportation service. Because of this requirement they were the last to arrive in the suburbs and lived by and la: ge in the innermost districts. This income group, the lower middle class, probably 20 to 30 percent of Boston's population, included the small shopkeepers, skilled artisans, the better-paid office and sales personnel, and the like. Many artisans' work locations changed frequently. Men in the building trades moved from job to job about the city; others, like machinists, cloth cutters, piano makers, printers, and furniture workers, moved from time to time to the different shops and factories of the city depending on which were busiest. For salesmen, clerks, and artisans alike the regular hours were long and most occupations had periodic or seasonal rush times when extra night or even Sunday work was required. Ambitious families who depended upon multiple employment for their advancement required a good central location for the home. Few members of this, the lowest and largest segment of Boston's middle class, could readily move beyond the limits of crosstown transportation service. Before the horsecar these men walked to work; in the 1870's and 1880's with the rising prosperity of the middle class and the growing efficiency of the streetcar they could travel through and around the central part of Boston for ten to sixteen cents a day. For such men to move beyond crosstown street railway service meant to greatly increase the time consumed in getting through the city and thereby to severely tax their ability to make a living.[2]

Since the lower middle class was the largest group of homeowners, in their parts of the metropolis building went forward at the most rapid rate. Throughout the last third of the nineteenth century those areas just beyond the periphery of the old walking city enjoyed the most rapid growth. Here lower middle class construction filled all the farms, estates, and vacant lots. Here land tended to be the most expensive of any in the suburbs because of the large numbers of residential bidders. Land values were further driven up by the presence of crosstown service which attracted industrial and commercial land buyers. Prices of land in Roxbury, inner Dorchester, and inner West Roxbury were perhaps 50 to 100 percent above those in the

Fig. 20. Some lower middle class suburban alternatives

outer areas of linear streetcar service and railroad commuting. On the other hand suburban land with crosstown service was probably but half the price of land in the intown tenement districts which lay next to the most expensive commercial and industrial land in the city.[3]

Thus the most numerous segment of the middle class, the group with the least income to devote to housing, had to pay the most for its land. In order to meet this cost, multiple dwellings, or very small single houses had to be resorted to. The jamming together of houses on small narrow lots characterized this group's building. Its principal architectural forms were the two-family house and the three-decker, a tall narrow detached wooden building of three apartments, one to a floor.

Though there were some similarities between the rich man's estate and the cheap two-families and three-deckers, the lesser product resembled its model in details only. The lots were so small and the pattern of living so dense that the rural setting was lost altogether. The advantages of incompletion, the rural atmosphere that came from only partial occupation of suburban land, now disappeared when high three-deckers moved onto vacant lots. Just as the cheap row houses and tenements of lower Tremont street were so pinched as to be mockeries of the ample formal style of the best South End town housing of the period preceding the Civil War, so the cramped suburban streets of three-deckers stand as an ugly joke against their models: the picturesque houses set on garden lots.

The growth of the transportation system influenced not only the kinds of houses built, but also their placement. The growing street railway system helped to create in Greater Boston areas of differing potential for new construction. The innermost region, the old walking city, was so built up by 1870 that the expansion of transportation service could only very slowly effect its new construction. In the region beyond the old walking city, however, there was plenty of space for new houses. Here the street railway changed the building potential of land according to the distinct transportation needs and income capabilities of each division of the upper-income half of the metropolitan population. The 1900 position of the bands of new construction, which were each one associated with a class division, can be seen in Map 9.

The band of the wealthy was at all times the farthest out, the largest in area, and the smallest in numbers of people. It was a zone of railroad service in which the streetcar played only a supplementary role even as late as 1900.[4] In 1870 this band of new construction for the wealthy fell within a radius from City Hall of 3.5 to 10 miles. By 1900 it had expanded and shifted outward so that it occupied a position 5 to 15 miles from City Hall. In this band farming continued and old villages remained, but sizeable quantities of land were taken up by the wealthy either for estates or as streets of large suburban homes. Today the visible remains of this band's former position can be seen in the Jamaica Pond section of West Roxbury, the Townsend street–Walnut avenue section of Roxbury highlands, and the Melville avenue–Carruth street and Savin Hill pockets of Dorchester. Because of a subsequent movement of cheaper construction into this outer band of expensive houses the old isolated structures of the wealthy have been obscured. The occasional estates and the patches of businessmen's "cottages" of the period 1840–1880, when Roxbury, West Roxbury, and Dorchester lay beyond good streetcar service, have been torn down or are so hemmed in as to be almost unrecognizable. Nevertheless, if one walks about the three towns looking for houses built before 1880 the image of former times emerges: scattered houses in a rural setting with a few prosperous streets connected to country villages. This was the form of the outer and wealthiest band of suburban building. The men who moved from Boston during these times were the only group

FIG. 21. Businessman's cottage; house 1846, picture 1878

FIG. 22. Lucy Stone House; house c. 1860, picture c. 1890

who got the setting that the ideology of the rural ideal demanded. In these years the communities were still small, the land plentiful, and the newcomers wealthy enough to build houses and gardens in a style consonant with their wishes.

For a number of reasons the street railway was extended to such sparsely settled areas. Probably most important was the desire of companies to prevent future competition. Horse-railway lines were inexpensive to lay compared to the steam railroad, and the costs of sending a car out to the farthest villages once an hour, or once every half hour, were also small. Some of these longest lines also had an interurban character. The addition of a few miles of track often meant connection to the lines of an outer industrial city. Thus, the long Neponset line in Dorchester connected with the Quincy trolleys.

Also, many of the founders and investors in street railways were real estate speculators who wanted to attract new customers for their land. Henry M. Whitney first established his West End line to Brookline for the sole purpose of promoting his Beacon street development. The Dorchester land speculators Nathan Carruth and Henry L. Pierce were both pioneer street-railway investors.

Finally, the special nineteenth century habit of Sunday rides to the parks and cemeteries outside the city made many of the most distant runs profitable. Until 1890 the suburban terminals at Grove Hall, Dorchester, and Forest Hills, West Roxbury, were situated on the edge of sparsely settled land. Their biggest day was Sunday, when thousands of Bostonians journeyed out from town to spend the day at the Castle Garden Amusement Park and nearby Franklin Park, or the Forest Hills Cemetery and Arnold Arboretum. With the establishment of metropolitan parks around the whole of Greater Boston in the 1890's, the farthest lines were pushed out to these new parks to take advantage of the Sunday traffic. Such lines encouraged building on metropolitan Boston's outer edges, near the beach sections of South Boston and Revere, and the park sections of Medford, Melrose, Newton, Dorchester, and West Roxbury.[5]

Once linear service was permanently established, the land through which it ran became a potential building area for the central middle class who built single and two-family houses. Their houses were either custom built or put up in small groups by speculative builders. The architecture was imitative of the most expensive fashions of the day, but money was lacking for lot and house sizes which could have made these designs as successful as their models.

There is no single rule of distance that describes the way land was taken up during this stage of transportation service, except to observe that middle class commuters spread themselves over the band of good linear service. Individual families building for themselves seem to have been a little more daring than the speculators: their houses appeared everywhere along the edge of established roads. Speculators, on the other hand, displayed a slight tendency in favor of building where land values were known, near established villages and closer to the intown edge of the linear service zone.

Both commercial house builders and individual families depended upon the prior work of land subdividers who cut up fields and laid out streets. The importance of this primary work cannot be overemphasized. The subdividers, by getting streets accepted as legal ways by the city of Boston, secured the modern water, gas, and sewer services so essential to small middle class developments. The main water and sewer lines, like the streetcar tracks, were run as rapidly as possible out to the principal suburban streets and thereby connected existing houses and villages with the central city system. Spurred by subdividers, the City of Boston completed the work begun by the streetcar companies. Together the streetcar service and the city utilities made every parcel within 200 and 500 yards of the old suburban streets potential building lots for the middle class.

The advantages of the suburb to residents of this second, middle class, band lay largely in its wide choice of home sites, and the factors of incompletion. The owners of these moderately priced houses could afford only relatively small lots, 4,000 to 6,000 square feet, but they enjoyed for a time the rural setting due to the presence of vacant fields and still-occupied estates that lay about their settlements.

In 1870 the band of new suburban construction for the central middle class lay in the area 2.5 to 3.5 miles from City Hall, although until the Depression of 1873 this group also continued building in the patterns of the walking city. The walking city districts of lower Roxbury and the South End were popular sites for new middle-income housing until 1873; then the central middle class shifted exclusively to suburban building. By 1900 the band of new construction for this income group had shifted from the area 2.5 to 3.5 miles from City Hall to an area 3.5 to 6 miles out.

In the three towns of Roxbury, West Roxbury, and Dorchester, the movement of this band of central middle class construction followed a somewhat irregular course. Its position at any moment depended upon the rate at which large parcels were offered for subdivision, and upon the proximity of villages which, as settlements increased, justified the establishment of crosstown service. The lower middle class tended to move into all areas where crosstown service was established and the lower middle class habits of building tended to push the central middle class construction farther out. During the building boom of the 1880's and 1890's the lower middle class began building in sections of outer Roxbury and nearby Dorchester where formerly central middle class construction had predominated.

The inner parts of Dorchester, lying as they did in the path of a ring of villages that stretched from South Boston through Dorchester to Roxbury and Brookline, justified crosstown service sooner than did central Dorchester. Central Dorchester was separated from the village of Jamaica Plain by Franklin Park, and it was part of a ring of widely distant villages that ran through Brookline to Newton and Brighton. Thus, linear service and the central middle class band of building lasted much longer in central Dorchester and in parts of West Roxbury than in the more intown districts. Because linear service lasted here for twenty years before the addition of crosstown service, much of central Dorchester and Jamaica Plain was filled with moderately priced singles and doubles. When crosstown service did come to this area there was little space left for lower middle class construction. The long duration of the linear street railway service was one factor in the relative stability of property values in these sections.

The streetcar network grew in a roughly radial fashion out from the center of Boston. As a result each addition of crosstown circumferential service was more difficult to add than the previous one, since circumferential routes grew so much longer with each mile traveled out along the inbound-outbound radius. The problems of the final limits of crosstown service never materialized in the nineteenth century since such progress as the streetcar made provided a substantial increase in land for all segments of the middle class. The radial arrangement of the street railway, however, allocated very different amounts of land to each group within the upper-income half of metropolitan Boston's population. Map 9, which shows the 1900 class bands of new construction, gives a good approximate view of the relative areas of land open to each class division.

In 1870 the wealthy were building in an enormous tract on the outer edge of the metropolis. The area of land within this 1870 band was fourteen times the area of the old walking city of 1850. By 1900

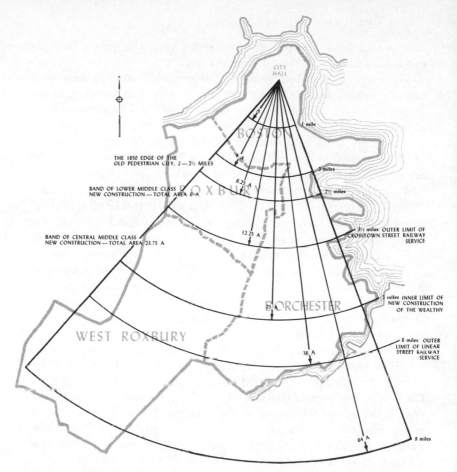

Map 9. Approximate class building bands of the three towns in 1900. A = 357.4 acres. It is the area of a 64-degree segment of a circle whose radius is one mile, roughly the distance from City Hall to Dover street. The other radii are marked in miles from Boston's City Hall, and their area is given in terms of A.

the band of construction for the wealthy had moved to a region 5 to 15 miles from Boston's City Hall. The potential area open to this group was now thirty-two times the old city.

The central middle class had less land at its disposal, but it enjoyed a very substantial increase in its allotment. In 1870 those members of the central middle class who were building in the suburbs occupied a band 2.5 to 3.5 miles from Boston. The outward movement of good linear street railway service and the shift of the central middle class to a predominant use of suburban styles gave this group twice as much land as it formerly was able to reach.

The lower middle class, because it depended upon crosstown street railway service, was confined to the inner parts of the segment of the metropolitan circle, and hence received much the smallest increment of land. In 1870 new lower middle class construction took place almost entirely within the confines of the old pedestrian city, in the West End, in inner South Boston, in East Boston, on the edges of the South End. By 1900 the expansion of crosstown street railway service had carried the band of lower middle class construction to a position 2.5 to 3.5 miles from City Hall. The gross area of this band was about equal to the area of the old walking city. The new land, however, was better than the old because it had been only partially built upon. Not only were there many open spaces for building but many houses in this region possessed large suburban lots which could be subdivided for further building. As a result, when the street railway brought crosstown service to the inner suburbs in the late 1880's and early 1890's it gave the lower middle class more land than it had ever commanded in the old pedestrian city.

If the streetcar with its further modification of rapid transit had not been succeeded in the 1920's by the automobile, perhaps a shortage of land like that affecting the walking city of the period preceding the Civil War might have developed. As it happened the progressive changes in transportation technology granted Boston's middle class a continuous enlargement of its supply of residential land. This abundance first began with the technological break made by the horsecar a hundred years ago and has continued without ceasing ever since. These successive transportation changes have made possible the shifting of fashions in middle class house lots from the first doubling of the walking city's row-house lots, to the parcels of 3,000–6,000 square feet common in the streetcar suburbs, to the present fashion of quarter- to full-acre, and even larger, lots. .

THE 1900 SEGREGATION

By 1900 the interaction of the growth of the street railway and class building patterns had produced class-segregated suburbs. As the bands of new construction moved ever outward they impressed upon the land their own special architectural and social patterns.

The band of lower middle class building and good crosstown street railway service had been roughly equivalent to the boundaries of the old town of Roxbury. Here during the thirty years from 1870 to 1900 cheap singles, doubles, and three-deckers had been jammed onto tiny lots. Within a limited and already partially occupied space of approximately 3 square miles the most numerous segment of the middle class had made its suburban home environment.

From 1870 to 1900 the band of good linear streetcar service had extended 3.5 to 6 miles from the center of the city; it included most of the towns of Dorchester and West Roxbury. Because of the radial arrangement of the streetcar lines this district held about 21 square miles of land and here more generous lot sizes had prevailed. Most commonly this area's new construction had taken the form of single and two-family houses for the central segment of the middle class, but there were also occasional streets and pockets of expensive upper middle class construction.

Of the 23,000 new residential buildings 38 percent had been built upon land of the inner band, 62 percent on the land of the outer zone. By 1900 the narrow confines of Roxbury were almost completely filled while the two towns of Dorchester and West Roxbury were only partially covered by commuters' houses.

Even the primitive statistics of the old state and federal censuses of the 1890's demonstrate the suburban divisions of the middle class. High-priced settlements included so few people that they were generally obscured by the large census areas of the day, but the division of the central and lower segments of the middle class invariably appear. Roxbury, with the exception of the highlands, was the home of lower middle class construction, and it showed a heavy concentration of small rental units, units of less rooms per family, and higher rents per room, than were common in the outer areas of Dorchester and West Roxbury. The higher rents reflected the competition for space in a district of crosstown streetcar service where the most populous segment of the middle class bid up land values. The smaller size of the units indicated the countervailing pressure of families of limited income keeping their total rent bills below those of more prosperous sections.

In a rough way occupational differences also appeared. In Roxbury there was a heavier concentration of those engaged in manufacture, and a smaller percentage of those in professions, than in the other towns.

Finally, the census showed the special suburban process of ethnic integration and income segregation. Early twentieth century observers called the inner suburbs the "zone of emergence." Here, first and second generation immigrant families moved from their original ethnic centers and began to take their place in the general life of the American middle class. In the 1870's and 1880's the Irish were Roxbury's largest emergent group. In the 1890's substantial numbers of Jews and Canadians began leaving the working class quarters of the old city.

Because of this habit of economic rise and outward migration the ethnic composition of suburbs often reflected the central city's population proportions of about thirty years previous. It took about a generation for a new immigrant group to form a large middle class population, about a generation for Irish, Jews, Canadians, or Germans to have substantial numbers of their national group living in the zones of new suburban construction.

The census also told something about the varying rates of movement of each nationality. The Germans, English, and Canadians— major components of Boston's old immigration—assimilated most rapidly and had heavier proportions of their numbers in the outer middle class suburbs than did the Irish or the Jews. Nevertheless, all immigrant aggregations, as predominantly groups with little property, began their life in the inner, low rent, sections of the city.[7]

Through the discipline of street railway transportation and the costs of new construction the suburbs displayed on an enlarged physical plan the dynamics of the metropolitan society. With the possibility for a more landed style of building Boston's middle class families abandoned the old central city and built new neighborhoods in the modern suburban, commuter, manner. In so doing they clustered together by their income capabilities and transportation needs so that the class divisions of the society came to be represented in large areas of similarly priced homes.

The income orientation of the new suburbs meant that the integration of Boston's immigrants took place roughly by generations. After one generation in the working class districts an immigrant group produced a substantial middle class which then joined other middle class families in the suburbs. The steady flow of new ethnic groups to the suburbs demonstrated the continued openness of the metropolitan society and its ability to provide a middle class competence to a big proportion of its immigrants' children.

CHAPTER FIVE

THE WEAVE OF SMALL PATTERNS

HAD THE land beyond Boston been absolutely vacant, had the new transportation and municipal services come to that land all on one day, and had there been but three different houses, each much more expensive than the last, then suburban Boston would have grown to a city of clearly visible concentric circles. Each section of the middle class would have been sharply separated from its neighboring section, and each would have lived successively farther from Boston. Early scholars of city growth like Burgess and Hoyt noted the tendency of classes to live in bands of circular or segmental patterns; this tendency, as we have seen, was directly related to the expansion of streetcar service.[1]

However, the houses in these bands were mixed in form and finely graded in price. There were cheap and expensive three-deckers, ample two-families that looked somewhat like expensive singles, and tiny single houses that were as cheap per family as most multiple dwellings. The land upon which houses were built varied widely in value because of its past use and prospective quality. The transportation service itself grew in an irregular and varied way so that here it retarded, there it accelerated, the flow of different income groups.

The Dorchester shore, though long served with good linear transportation, remained for twenty-five years a section of little building. In Roslindale from 1886 to 1896, at least a mile beyond other moderately priced dwellings, a large cluster of houses sprang up. The outer parts of the Tremont street district, between Tremont and Centre streets in Roxbury, developed late and in the lower middle class pattern. Roxbury highlands, though surrounded on three sides by lower middle class construction from 1887 on, continued for years to receive expensive and moderately priced houses. The history of each section of the suburbs was affected by such things as: speculation in property with a marine potential, geographic conditions that influenced transportation and utility routes, the presence of old manufacturing clusters, and the tenacity of older fashions.

The Depression of 1873 was of considerable consequence to settlement patterns. In 1873 there began a twelve-year slack period in suburban construction, but these bad times only briefly checked the expansion of the street railway. As a result of this divergence between the building cycle and the progress of transportation, when the residential building boom recommenced in the mid-1880's the zone of lower middle class building of the crosstown streetcar service stage overlaid a partially completed section of the linear stage. Many Roxbury and inner Dorchester neighborhoods beginning to be settled with substantial singles and two-families were suddenly inundated with cheap construction. Most of the merits of the earlier form of building were buried, and a potential area of rapid deterioration was established.

As a result of historic conditions and different building practices, suburban building during the last third of the nineteenth century went forward in a more mixed and variable pattern than today. It was after all a period without zoning, without large-scale builders, and without public control of subdivision. The degree of discipline of the thousands of small builders who made the decisions to build houses and the degree of variation among the patterns of their work can best be demonstrated by an examination of the histories of some small districts within the towns. Three quite different districts have been chosen for such examination: central Dorchester, the Tremont street district, and Roxbury highlands.

Central Dorchester was an area of about four square miles of rolling uplands. It represented about one half of the town of Dorchester and was in the late nineteenth century a major site of single and two-family construction. This district is perhaps the best example of the interaction of the development of transportation and new construction. Moreover, it displays the strong ethnic integrating force of the new suburbs.

The Tremont street district of Roxbury was a partially filled settlement of the old pre-streetcar metropolis. During the last half of the nineteenth century it was rapidly built up to cheap construction. The area constitutes a record of the habits of lower middle class building, and reveals the unstable nature of this, the most usual, kind of suburban building.

Roxbury highlands was a medium- to high-priced quarter. The unique qualities of this district test the power of neighborhood conditions to retard the general flow of classes and show that neighborhood influence could at most delay for thirty years the general metropolitan patterns of population movement.

Central Dorchester

Decisions made years before Boston commuters arrived on the scene defined the field of choice open to them. From the joint influence of geography and history came a kind of regulation of building that was often tantamount to zoning. The geographical inheritance of Dorchester did much to prepare the town for its late nineteenth century building boom. Its rolling uplands had early attracted farmers. In subsequent years these farm fields proved easy to build houses on. With the exception of a few steep hills and some marshes by the ocean and by the Neponset River, the town presented no special site problems. Before the streetcar lines Dorchester had been isolated from Boston by the South Bay; but with the establishment of good transportation in the 1880's the town's land was suddenly thrown open to mass development.

Dorchester's building tracts were large in comparison to the patchwork activity in contemporary Roxbury and West Roxbury where unevenness of the land, previous heavy settlements, and the presence of large parks caused construction to be limited to small pockets. When good linear streetcar service reached out into central Dorchester in the 1870's and 1880's the old farms filled up with middle-income housing.[2] Here in an area at least seven times the size of its more famous contemporary, the Back Bay, there sprang up in twenty years a section of houses of fairly narrow price range. Because of its size the district has been able to maintain its homogeneity and to survive later shifts in its population without more than partial encroachment by cheap housing forms.

Had geographic conditions prevented this middle-income tract from being so large, or had sizeable pockets of land remained undeveloped, substantial proportions of lower priced housing would have moved into the tract in the late nineties and early twentieth century when cross-

Fig. 23. Central Dorchester, 1903; Ceylon street from Bird

town street railway service was instituted. In such an event the structural homogeneity of the area would have been destroyed. Many of the middle class families who first built there would probably have abandoned it and the character of the section would have shifted rapidly. However, because by 1900 it was both large and well filled with moderate statements of the day's housing fashion, central Dorchester has run down gradually through the movement of generations rather than from any sudden exodus of an ethnic or income group.

Dorchester's geography also had other consequences for its suburban development. The town's two principal villages, the seventeenth century one at Meeting House Hill and the eighteenth century Second Parish at Washington street and Talbot avenue, lay centered on the inner and outer farm areas. The transmission of this early organization of the town's land to later generations constitutes one of the major elements in the informal zoning of late nineteenth century central Dorchester.

The roads that connected the two early villages to each other and to the villages of Roxbury, Quincy, Hyde Park, Dedham, and Boston were not random cowpaths but rational links for a farming community. The roads, like the villages, accommodated themselves to the contours of the land and served a maximum number of farms with

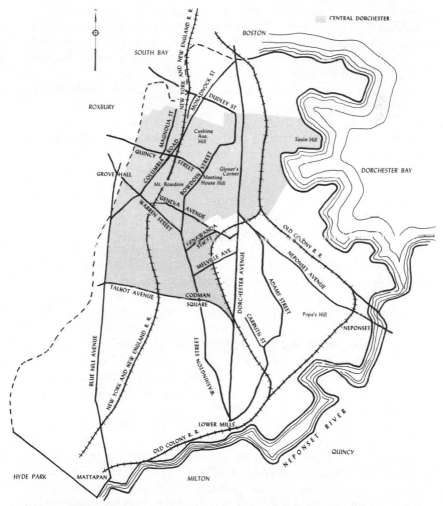

MAP 10. Dorchester. Central Dorchester is an arbitrary division of the town set by the author for his convenience in plotting the location of new construction.

the least miles of road. The influence of these roads and villages was perpetuated by the steam railroads which connected the existing villages, and by the street railways and the sewer, water, gas, and electric mains which used these roads or close parallels to them.

First to come were the railroads. Though the residents of Dorchester opposed steam trains as a hazard to life and property and a menace to the rural peace of the town, the Old Colony Railroad instituted service along the Dorchester shore between Quincy and Boston in 1845. Ten years later the New York and New England[3] established an upland service through central Dorchester between Readville and Boston.

Railroad engineers had two interests when locating their tracks. One was to keep the grades as gradual as possible; the other, to run the tracks in such a way as to pick up the most traffic. As a result, Dorchester's lines, and indeed all the railroad lines of the three towns, follow the contours between the villages much as did the old roads. The Old Colony followed the shore line to connect up the lowland villages. The New York and New England, a late arrival, was forced to take the steeper upland route, but it ran along reasonably level farm lands and built stations at such rural clusters as existed.

In this way railroad construction reinforced the former village location patterns. The first upper middle class railroad commuters established clusters at or close to the settlements of the older farming community. Their role was thus to continue the patterns of the past and transmit them, along with a demonstration of the new suburban way of life, to the next group of builders—the central segment of the middle class.

The good linear streetcar service and full-scale sanitation and utility services, which came to be offered in central Dorchester during the 1880's, also followed the logic of the railroad engineers, and in so doing reinforced the old traffic patterns. From these cumulative effects of geographic arrangement and historical events there grew up in Dorchester one large tract suitable for medium-priced construction. Based on the town's old farm road and village pattern, the tract stretched from Upham's Corner to Codman Square, from Blue Hill avenue to Dorchester avenue. The half of Dorchester that was not suitable to large-scale medium-priced building was made up of industrial and marsh tracts that bordered the South and Dorchester bays, and the outer section of the town, which, during the last third of the nineteenth century, lay beyond easy commuting distance to Boston.[4]

Fig. 24. Professional builder's middle-priced single, 1880

The results of this *de facto* zoning of central Dorchester manifested themselves both in the structures that were built and the people who lived in them. By 1900, after thirty years of active building, the wooden detached single and two-family houses ruled the area.[5] Most houses occupied long narrow lots of 3,000 to 6,000 square feet, and the neat suburban street lined with trees and small lawns was almost universal. Such blocks can be seen today, especially in the outer sections of central Dorchester, the parts that were built up rapidly in the 1885–1895 boom. In the older, partly settled, inner parts of central Dorchester, land came on the market in small parcels, and a block often took twenty to thirty years to be completed. Here, there is today often a display of the thirty-year progress of architectural ornament, and often, too, a considerable variety in the basic forms of the houses.

The main traffic streets of 1900 presented the greatest structural variety. Until the electrification of streetcars in 1889 and 1890 brought the noise of grinding steel to these streets, arterial lots were the most popular and the most expensive. They were also the most convenient and the easiest to develop. Here, railroad commuters had

Fig. 25. Single-family house, 1885

first built their houses on large square lots; but by 1900 rows of stores, frequently stores with apartments above, and tall narrow three-deckers had taken the spaces between the old houses.

Multiple structures pre-empted main streets, and on any given street there were sometimes both cheap and expensive single and two-family houses, and even an occasional three-decker. Nevertheless, compared to the older parts of Boston, central Dorchester was over-whelmingly the place of the singles and doubles of the central segment of the middle class. There were few of the very smallest singles, no narrow alleys, few cheap three-deckers or tenements. Even after 1890 when crosstown street railway service opened the inner half of central Dorchester to lower middle class building, the preponderance of new construction continued for at least a decade in moderately priced structures. Whatever the structure, families of this section had larger interior space, in comparison to neighboring lower middle class districts, as well as a moderate level of rents and a neighborhood of little grass plots and small garden spaces.

The influence of the street railway, important as it was to the development of central Dorchester, did not by itself determine the district's history. The uniform character of central Dorchester was also achieved through the action of common understanding within the society as to what constituted appropriate kinds of buildings for different areas and different incomes. The new suburbs were a society of tradesmen, salesmen, small manufacturers, professionals, and artisans, men working hard to make a good living and to get ahead. It is not surprising that these men built their houses by the same measure as they judged themselves.

The tendency of families to seek out neighbors with incomes similar to their own exerted a strong force toward the building and maintaining of structurally and economically homogeneous districts. This uniformity continued in some cases even in the face of potential price competition for the land. Builders for the lower middle class, using small lots and multiple structures, could have outbid middle class and

Fig. 26. Two-family house, 1894

upper middle class buyers in most of the subdivisions of central Dorchester.[6] Nevertheless, large numbers of lower middle class houses were not built in the inner section until at least the 1890's and the outer part until the twentieth century. The informal regulation of building in central Dorchester seems largely to have been the product of the desire of families to build near other families of their "kind," and most families seem to have been reluctant to go far beyond the boundaries of established class neighborhoods.

In addition to this clustering of people with like incomes there were some special building practices that tended to keep an area architecturally and economically homogeneous. Both homeowners, who purchased a single lot for a custom-built house, and professional builders, who handled several lots at a time, sought safety for their investment by building dwellings of a type common to the area. In this way an architectural and income uniformity continued from year to year until there was a radical shift in transportation or expansion of an adjacent neighborhood to bring large numbers of a different income into the area.

No special regulatory body was needed to tell most builders what was appropriate; the other houses in the area presented them with models. Thus, in the years between substantial shifts in transportation or architectural style neighborhoods continued building in uniform patterns.

The practice of repetitive building was assisted by the habits of late nineteenth century speculative builders. They were a conservative group and sought safety in their operations by restricting themselves to one or two house styles and catering to a limited price range of customer. Once a builder had learned a successful land-house combination he stuck to it until fashion forced him to abandon it. If the area he worked in shifted its character, so that his kind of operation was no longer the popular one, he usually preferred to move to new land rather than to vary his house and land style.

Shifts in the housing form of an area—the change from singles and doubles to three-deckers, the substitution of cheap for expensive types in each form—were frequently accompanied by the coming of a different set of builders. The outward migration of the three segments of the middle class was attended by a similar migration of builders. In thirty-years time builders moved from the South End, to lower Roxbury, to Dorchester, and even to Brookline, following the opening of land suitable to the segment of the middle class they catered to. Even though there were no zoning laws and no mass builders who put up whole communities in a few years, this repetitive habit of little builders produced an effect somewhat similar to the modern class-graded residential suburbs.

There were three principal exceptions to structural uniformity in the suburbs. The first was the dwelling and store unit which appeared as a wooden or brick tenement with stores on the first floor. The commercial possibilities of land on the main arteries and at railroad stations encouraged these buildings whose cramped quarters were clearly out of harmony with the style of living of the rest of the new suburban houses.

The second exception to uniformity came from pockets of undesirable land that were scattered through every section. Near factories, on swampy and rough spaces, occasional cheap singles were built for lower middle class owners who were willing to move beyond the main

FIG. 27. Neighborhood dwelling and store unit, c. 1880

Fig. 28. Lower middle class minimum-priced single, c. 1870

body of their income group and who wished to avoid multiple dwellings.[7]

The third, and by far the most numerous incongruity, derived from business failure and the pressure upon small capitalists to liquidate the uncompleted fragments of their projects. Most frequently the odds and ends of a subdivision would be sold off for three-deckers, or cheap doubles, or the land would be redivided into small lots to attract purchasers who had only a little to pay for land. Many of the incongruities of central Dorchester derive from this process, not from a later influx of lower class families brought by a shift in transportation.[8]

Many times these incongruities in structure were more architectural than economic, for rents in a new three-decker could be as high or higher than those of older singles and doubles located on the same street. An 1891 study shows but slight variations in Dorchester rents. There was no premium space and the few really cheap rentals were restricted to the old mill villages. This study indicates that within most of Dorchester's new suburban population gradations in ability to pay were small.[9] Nevertheless, the pressure on small speculators to sell off their odd parcels did hasten the stage of complete occupancy of the land, a stage that ended the advantages of incompletion which were so desirable to middle-income families seeking a somewhat rural setting without the means to purchase large lots.

The custom of repetitive building, created by construction practices and supported by transportation service, laid out wide areas of partially settled land where middle-income families could choose to live. In these areas of similar incomes the integration of the various ethnic elements of the middle class took place. Nationality and occupational statistics when taken together show Dorchester to have been a middle-income community whose ethnic composition reflected the steady rise of new immigrants into the middle class. In 1880 foreign born and their children contributed 46.3 percent of the town's population; in 1905, 57.3 percent. This increase by 11 percent corresponds with the experience of other suburban areas, and the experience of the city of Boston as a whole. An increase of 10 to 15 percent in the proportion of the foreign born and their children was usual for the period.

The full explanation of these changes lies in the timing of the Irish, Italian, and Jewish immigration, and the relative speed with which these groups entered middle class American society as compared to Canadian, English, and Scottish immigrants. Foreign immigrants came to the city, like the country Americans, to make their fortunes, and it took them time to establish themselves on an equal footing with those already there. In comparison to native Americans all immigrant groups were more concentrated in the inner, low-income sections of the city and the suburbs. The Canadians, who in Boston were almost entirely English-speaking, and the Scots and English were most at home in the society. Both the 1880 and the 1905 censuses show the relative ease with which they merged into the native population and diffused throughout the whole suburban band of the metropolis. The enormous Irish peasant population acquired the wherewithal for suburban living and the desire to mix with the whole society with less readiness. However, by 1880 there was an extensive Irish middle class in Boston. In that year 10 percent of Dorchester's population were Irish-born; 20 percent, children of Irish immigrants.

In 1905 the town was split into three wards: a combined Dorchester–South Boston ward, a ward that covered most of the new central Dorchester building, and an outer ward. The census shows the Irish to have been evenly spread through each of these wards, making up about 25 percent of the population in each. The 5 percent loss in the

Irish proportion of the town's population during the years 1880–1905 was a consequence of the decline of Irish immigration during the late nineteenth century and the disappearance of the third generation into the census category of native born. As new immigrant groups came to Boston they took their place behind the Irish in the steady flow from the central city. The Dorchester statistics of 1905 show a great inrush of Canadians and the beginning of the appearance of Russian and German Jews.[10]

The real estate atlases of the late nineteenth century display the migration of peoples with great clarity. Almost every street in Dorchester contained at least one landowner from each of the major immigrant groups. There were concentrations, to be sure, but these concentrations were but eddies in the steady flow of the middle class; they were temporary aggregations only. Such clusters as existed can be termed temporary and subsidiary to the main integrating flow of ethnically mixed income groups because their life span was so short and their influence so limited. Just as the time span from the building to the beginning decline of central Dorchester's single and two-family house district was but twenty to thirty years, so likewise its ethnic concentrations endured the same number of years.

Though an Irish, German, Canadian, or old Yankee group might concentrate at a point and secure its situation with the establishment of a church, clubs, and a school, these clusters always remained subservient to the outward migration of Boston's middle class. The fate of the cluster depended upon the economic progress of the ethnic group as a whole, not upon the success or failure of its institutions in maintaining a unified community.

The local church and its collateral institutions might endure for 50 years, or even 250 years, but throughout that time its parishioners shifted in social and economic status as did the land they occupied. Since the nineteenth century was eminently an era of immigration the various income clusters contained different ethnic proportions, and therefore every shift in the income level of a neighborhood included an ethnic shift.

Beyond the effects of changed transportation, which could suddenly change the income levels of small residential districts, the creation and destruction of ethnic concentrations depended upon the workings of housing obsolescence. An established ethnic cluster often retarded the effects of obsolescence by continuing to attract a higher range of incomes than an aging neighborhood would ordinarily have been able to do.

Because of the constant supply of new land brought forth by the expansion of the streetcar system, standards for lot sizes rose continually throughout the 1870–1900 period. These rising requirements for land, which were accompanied by periodic shifts in architecture, accelerated the obsolescence of new and partially completed neighborhoods. In a period of such rapid change it was not the fashion leaders who built on vacant lots in sections where the majority of houses were ten to twenty years old. Rather, such new home builders were families seeking to attach themselves to seemingly secure and established conditions.

From the logic of things it seems most reasonable to assume that latecomers would probably be of a lower income level than their predecessors, that latecomers would have made their choice out of limited income, inexperience, and lack of knowledge of the possibilities. However, there is considerable evidence that such was not always the case. The existence of an ethnic cluster, a private or parochial school, or a fashionable church might attract families of a considerable range of income into an obsolescent neighborhood.

The 1870–1900 Irish cluster that grew up around Meeting House Hill, with the parish of St. Peter's church was such a case. For a time this part of central Dorchester survived the changes in transportation which ultimately transformed the whole area into a lower middle class suburb. The section was the historic Yankee village of Dorchester. Here on the village green stood, and still stands, a typical New England Church. Next door was the neo-classic Lyceum, a similar monument to the Yankee era of the 1840's. In this building the first Masses of the neighborhood were said. In the 1840's and 1850's the hills about the green afforded a fine prospect of the farms of the town and the bay beyond. Railroad commuters began to move to the area and their houses dotted the hills and clustered along the main village roads.

By 1870 several estate owners had cut up their land for house lots. Speculators and individual homeowners alike were putting up moderately priced singles all over the neighborhood.[11] One speculator, a local Republican politician, became so confident of the village's growth that in 1880 he put up a row of 35 town houses. There is some reason to believe that he mistook a building boom at the advent of a streetcar suburb for the coming of the South End; such mistakes were charac-

Fig. 29. Meeting House Hill, First Parish Church (Unitarian), and Lyceum Hall in 1900

teristic of the beginning years of suburban development. Few people realized the full import of the continuously expanding supply of land which the streetcar would bring.[12]

This whole inner Dorchester zone was also of a more mixed architectural character than later outer districts because by 1870 much of the land was in the hands of railroad commuters. These families sold out and moved off slowly so that parcels came on the market in small patches all over the district. Unlike outer Dorchester, most streets contain a variety of different age and style houses. On Monadnock and Magnolia streets and on the hills to the south of Meeting House Hill, there are full streets of 1890 single and double houses but these are not the rule. More usual are streets like Quincy, or the streets off Bowdoin street, where a patch of 1870 singles is followed by high grade 1900 three-deckers after which come a few 1885 doubles and singles, then perhaps a railroad commuter's old single on the remains of an old square lot, followed by a row of cheap 1890 three-deckers.

The role of the Irish in this district of mixed structures was to continue building more expensive houses than the transportation pattern would have justified for an equivalent income group of another ethnic

origin. The Irish first moved to the area at Glover's Corner, just below
Meeting House Hill. Presumably these settlers of the 1840–1870 period
were an extension of the middle class Irish community of inner South
Boston which, though some distance away, shared the same Dorchester avenue transportation route to Boston. It was for this group that
Masses were first said at the Lyceum. By the 1870's horsecar service
had opened this whole area up to settlers from Roxbury and the South
End as well as those from South Boston. With this influx, instead of a
small chapel for the Glover's Corner group as was planned, the parish
priest was able to build a large church on the green at Meeting House
Hill. By the 1880's St. Peter's was one of the most active and prosperous parishes in Boston.[13]

Fig. 30. Meeting House Hill, St. Peter's Roman Catholic
Church in 1903

Fig. 31. Expensive houses, Magnolia street, Dorchester in the 1890's

In economic terms the Irish community of inner Dorchester during the 1870's and 1880's seems to have possessed the same income range as the Protestant group that was mixed among it. However, the presence of a high quality parochial school and fashionable church acted as a magnet to hold the upper segments of the Irish middle class even after the area was no longer fashionable for the middle class as a whole. St. Peter's of Dorchester in this way delayed class movement in much the same way as did the Roxbury Latin School and Protestant churches of Roxbury highlands.

For a time in the 1890's there grew up around St. Peter's the beginnings of an all middle class Irish community with a variety of housing types appropriate to the varied economic capabilities of the families in the parish. For example, in 1887 a wealthy contractor, Neil McNeil, built for himself an expensive house in the best Newport, Rhode Island, manner. It sat on an acre of land on top of the Stanley Street hill. At the bottom of this same short street he put up three-deckers for the less prosperous. However, elsewhere he did not practice mixing. In Roxbury highlands he built single family houses on streets already established in this pattern. In so doing, McNeil was following the regular procedure of the outer suburbs where homeowners and speculators alike put up streets of houses in a uniform style and income range.

The new outer areas were also being occupied by the Irish at the same time St. Peter's parish was settled. In the new mixed ethnic neighborhoods they built Catholic churches in the latest architecture next to similar Protestant churches. The McNeils continued to live in inner Dorchester but the new men of their economic standing moved outward. They were drawn to suburbs of uniform class structure, plentiful land, and up-to-date styles. The mixed building pattern of St. Peter's parish meant many singles were darkened by three-deckers or had been cramped onto too small lots. These conditions were satisfactory to a generation fresh from the South End and other parts of inner Boston, but their children knew and wanted better.[14]

In 1895 good crosstown streetcar service ran through mid-Dorchester. The lower middle class began to move into St. Peter's parish. It approached the neighborhood from three sides, from Dudley street,

Fig. 32. Neil McNeil's Newport style mansion, 1887

from the side streets off Blue Hill avenue, and from Dorchester avenue. One large part of this lower segment of the middle class was newly emergent Jews who had no need for either St. Peter's or the old First Church. Most of the newcomers were a lower income group of Canadians and Irish who took up the vacant land for three-deckers and apartments, and converted singles into multiple dwellings. Both Catholic and Protestant parishes continued, and are active to this day, but they serve a lower middle and working class population. Just like the old houses themselves, the church structures and institutions built to the needs of a rising middle class must now be transformed to serve purposes for which they were never designed. Moreover, these institutions face their task of defining a good and moral life for their parishioners in the midst of an area no longer regarded by the bulk of the middle class as an adequate environment for family life.

Tremont Street District

Despite some important exceptions all of West Roxbury and Dorchester during the years 1870 to 1900 belonged to families of the central segment of the middle class. It was their land, and in thirty years they covered with their new streets and houses about half of its twenty-one square miles of privately held land. As their class grew in numbers, as fashions changed, or as old neighborhoods became unsatisfactory, they moved steadily outward over still vacant suburban land. The new parks, cemeteries, churches, schools, and clubs were theirs also, for these institutions depended upon the central segment of the middle class for continued use and support in order to maintain the kinds of service for which they had been established.

Lower Roxbury, the major part of the town after the highlands has been excepted,[15] was, on the other hand, the land of the lower middle class. Others lived there to be sure. There were long residents from the days when Roxbury was a peripheral town—early suburbanites and employees of nearby mills. But lower middle class families were the driving force of this part of Roxbury. They built the new houses that sheltered the majority of the 43,000 newcomers to the district. And they did their building on an area of three square miles. This three square miles had been established by 1870 as a peripheral town of the Boston metropolis, and held a population of about 22,000. Within this narrow compass lower middle class families had to erect their version of the rural ideal.[16]

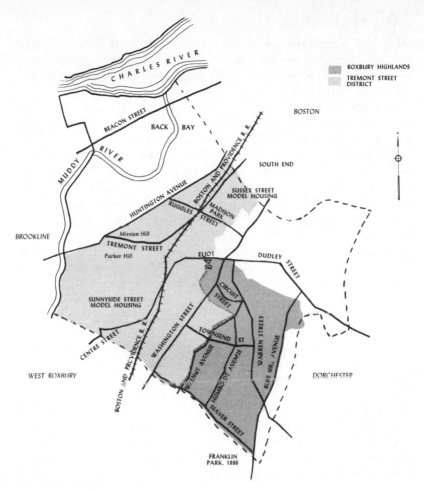

MAP 11. Roxbury. The Tremont street district and Roxbury highlands are arbitrary divisions of the town set by the author for his convenience in plotting the location of new construction.

In some ways it seems ridiculous to mention the rural ideal in connection with such a narrow and mean form of building as that which went up in lower Roxbury in the late nineteenth century. This was, above all, the land of the possible, not the ideal. Though customers for new houses were many, their means were sharply limited; the work had to be closely financed, closely figured, and built fast. Almost half the new dwelling construction of the three towns of Roxbury, West Roxbury, and Dorchester went on in this small area. Many men made a steady living out of this kind of construction, but of those builders about whose lives something is known, the overwhelming proportion of those trapped into bankruptcy or forced mortgage sales worked in this risky and highly competitive price range.[17]

Like the moderately priced houses of Dorchester and West Roxbury, the houses in lower Roxbury were built from stock plans and with stock ornament. Unlike the middle-priced construction, there was here little money for an extra bay, a large porch, or a shifting about of the builder's sketches. Most lower middle class families building or buying a new house asked, "how much for how little?" The streets of three-deckers, cramped two-families and brick row houses represent what were thought to be the best buys of the day. At least 56.9 percent of the new buildings of lower Roxbury were multiple structures. These structures were owned by a family living in them, or, more usually, by some landlord of the immediate neighborhood who had put his savings in this kind of investment.[18]

If one considers the new construction of lower Roxbury in comparison to other equivalent structures, the value of this cheap building becomes clear. By and large the new streets of Roxbury were well laid out with an eye to being easy to get through and easy to clean. Each house had a full set of modern plumbing facilities, gas for light and often gas stoves as well, and, toward the end of the century, electric lights. Many new houses had central heat. In most cases the principal rooms were larger than those of the contemporary West End tenement or the rooms in South End row housing. Compared to the old wooden mill barracks of Roxbury the new three-deckers and two-families were extravagant of space. Generally all rooms in a rental unit had outside windows and many had sunlight and good ventilation. Where three-deckers and two-families were jammed together on narrow lots, as was frequently the case, much light and air was lost and conditions approached those of the old row housing. However, in much of the new Parker Hill district and in patches everywhere in Roxbury lot sizes were adequate, and the light, air, and green space allotment of the new houses exceeded that of the contemporary Back Bay house.[19]

These essential characteristics of the new housing of Roxbury were all gains in the necessaries of family life. One of the most important achievements of suburban building during the last three decades of the nineteenth century was that, even in its cheapest housing forms, it

Fig. 33. Lower middle class housing, the walking city c. 1850

represented an advance over previous city conditions. The new lower
middle class neighborhoods constituted an important step toward
providing a safe, sanitary environment for all the families of Boston.
This general rise in minimum standards for new housing owes most
of its progress to the increase in size and in buying power of the middle
class and the contemporary public health and sanitation movement
which was actively supported by that class.

Nevertheless, the rural ideal, which was present in all levels of middle class thought, definitely influenced the forms new construction
took. The lower middle class streets and structures were a part of one
continuous spectrum of building style. If you walk today through
Roxbury and Dorchester you will notice only slight changes from
street to street in ornament, house, and lot styles. Most apparent are
shifts from single-family houses to three-deckers. Since the lower middle class built in areas often already developed many of the streets of
their part of nineteenth century Roxbury are mixed in types of structures. For this reason it is only after going some distance from an area
of decidedly lower-price to one of decidedly higher-price building that

Fig. 34. The walking city styles carried to the suburbs, 1873: numbers 1485–1495 Columbus avenue, Roxbury

you will notice a very definite change in a district's quality of plan and building. The sharpest break in house style and lot arrangement came not between the middle- and lower-priced housing but between the medium-priced and the expensive. Big houses, elaborate ornament, and expensive materials sharply distinguish an occasional street of the wealthy from the rest of the suburbs.

Since the kinds of houses appropriate to a rural setting provided most of the architectural inspiration, these styles necessarily underwent severe changes under the cramped conditions of a cheap suburban location. The landscaped rural garden and fields became a miniscule backyard, or almost disappeared altogether; the back porch and front stoop were all that remained of summer houses and shaded verandas. Today a street of three-deckers resembles nothing so much as the old row housing. But in the nineties the same street, with its tended trees and cultivated back yards, its location near the new parks and adjacent to neighborhoods of adequate yards, was an important step toward suburban life. Also, excepting one special case in lower Roxbury,[20] almost all new construction after 1873 took the form of detached houses. Again, there was a slavish copying of each shift in style in more expensive construction. All these elements point to a building process that shared one common stylistic motivation—the rural ideal.

Architecture was not the only quality held in common by the lower, central, and upper segments of the middle class. Like more expensive residences, the placement of lower middle class structures depended upon the street railway. In large measure the dependence of the group upon crosstown service, and the relatively limited range of that service, caused the crowded land patterns of its building. Income segregation also dominated its neighborhoods. Dense building habits drove out families of higher income who had first settled the land to enjoy the quasi-rural setting of the suburbs, while the costs of new construction kept most working class families out of these dis-

Fig. 35. A lower middle class suburban alternative, minimum-priced three-deckers of the 1890's

tricts. Finally, lower middle class neighborhoods provided an environment for the integration of families of similar income and diverse ethnic background. As in all other suburban areas, ethnic clusters of the lower middle class were temporary and dependent upon the general progress of immigrant families in the metropolitan society as a whole.

Beyond its demonstration of the uniformity of behavior at all levels of suburban construction, lower middle class building had special attributes which were of great consequence to the future of the metropolis. Lower middle class families, who depended upon crosstown transportation, were generally the last to arrive in any suburb. Because they were the final builders, their work gave a permanent set to the residential environment. The wealthy and the central segment of the middle class occupied great tracts of land, but only partially covered them. In most of their settlements plenty of room remained for new houses. When the lower middle class moved in force into a neighborhood, sheer weight of numbers brought a complete occupancy of the land. Since the terminal users of houses, the working class, were too poor to build new structures, these later generations were restricted to the inheritance of what had gone before. In this way the narrow means of lower middle class families became a permanent condition for much of the housing of the metropolis.

Limited financial ability brought two special qualities to lower middle class building: first, it crowded the land and thereby prevented later adaptation to the changing incomes and needs of its residents; second, it led a great many houses to be built to specifications which were below the common understanding of what constituted a satisfactory home. Such building was accepted by contemporaries as the best alternative of the moment, but it immediately fell to obsolescence upon any substantial change in home finance, income distribution, transportation service, or housing fashions.

The inflexibility and compromised quality of much lower middle class construction in the end gave it a destructive role in the process of city building. First it destroyed the character of existing neighborhoods by its jamming of the land, and, later, it destroyed its own good qualities by being inadaptable to future requirements. Both the general characteristics of lower middle class building and its special destructive qualities are well demonstrated by the history of the Tremont street district of lower Roxbury.

In 1870 this section was divided in two parts: a well settled area near the South End of Boston, and a lightly settled outer part which included Mission and Parker hills. Though the outer part enjoyed good linear streetcar service it had, by 1870, failed to become as well filled with houses as equivalent sections of Dorchester. The presence of factories in the nearby Stony Brook Valley and the steepness of the hill grades had inhibited its development. Its moment of mass building awaited the results of the annexation of Roxbury to Boston, namely, complete town coverage by water, street, sewer, and gas service, without regard to the height or grade of any lot.

The inner district was partly a less expensive continuation of South End middle-income housing, partly the residence of factory hands who worked in nearby Roxbury and South End industries. Also, because downtown Boston lay only a mile and a half away, men living here could walk to most of the employment centers of the pre-streetcar metropolis. Because of its convenience, during the years 1840 to 1870 the inner parts of the Tremont street district grew rapidly in the mixed form of the old peripheral towns.

The more prosperous lived in tiny classic revival wooden single and double houses, and in the brick tenement and store buildings that were put up along the busy Tremont street thoroughfare. On the side streets factory owners had erected two-and-a-half- and three-story wooden barracks for their employees. Up toward Mission Hill and on the flats near Ruggles street, cheap wooden houses and brick rows of the 1860's and 1870's were the general rule. On the edge of the then unfilled Back Bay marshes there were also an indeterminate number of shacks belonging to the shanty Irish poor.[21]

This inner section of Roxbury developed with a great concentration of Irish immigrants and as the colony grew it spread with heavy concentration over the whole of Mission Hill, Parker Hill, and lower Jamaica Plain. This same area during the years 1840 to 1870 held a large German group which worked in the breweries and factories of the adjacent Stony Brook Valley and South End. The German colony prospered during the last third of the nineteenth century and, like the rest of the central middle class, migrated out from the city. In 1900 its center was in Roslindale, three miles up the Stony Brook Valley from its 1870 inner Roxbury location. The German group founded the church on Mission Hill, a church which, like St. Peter's in Dorchester, gave cohesion to the cluster which grew up around it.

Fig. 36. Working class barracks, c. 1850; picture taken during the great Stony Brook flood of 1886

Fig. 37. Working class housing, lower Roxbury, during the flood of 1886

Until 1846 there was no Roman Catholic church in Roxbury. Then, in the same year that Roxbury became a city, St. Joseph's Church on Circuit and Regent streets was established to serve the Catholics of Roxbury, Dorchester, Brookline, Hyde Park, Dedham, and Norwood. This site was well chosen. It lay in a new middle class section of Roxbury highlands close to the Tremont street thorough-fare and the intersection of the main arteries of Washington, Dudley, and Warren streets. By 1870 parish churches had been, or were about to be, established in all of these towns while the growth of the Catholic, especially Irish, population in Roxbury demanded new churches.

The most important of the new churches from the point of view of the development of the Tremont street district was the Redemptorist Mission Church opened in 1871 on Mission Hill at Tremont and St. Alphonsus streets. The estate purchased for the church was an historic Roxbury site. It was General Artemus Ward's Revolutionary War headquarters, the estate of General Henry Dearborn of the War of 1812, the home of his extravagant son, General Henry A. S. Dearborn who is known for his part in designing the Mount Auburn and Forest Hills cemeteries. To this same house the Ursulines had come and had stayed for a time after the Charlestown riot and the burning of their convent. The old estate, however, had, like the whole neighborhood, fallen from the heights of fashion; for the few years prior to its purchase by the Catholic Church it served as a pleasure resort. Since 1873 the new stone Church of Our Lady of Perpetual Help has looked down over the Back Bay toward the North End. Both literally and figuratively it served as a beacon for lower middle class Irish families emerging from the tenements of Boston.

In 1870 most of Roxbury's 5,000 Irish lived in the inner part of town. Many of these were poor families attracted to pockets of cheap marshy land located on the periphery of Boston settlement. In the next thirty years such families continued to come to Roxbury where they took up old houses abandoned by middle-income groups. These families could not afford to buy new houses or pay the rents required by any but the most mean and crowded new tenement. Their presence in lower Roxbury kept down the social status of the land.[22]

The effect of the Redemptorist Church with its popular ritual and full set of parochial services was to attract a different group of Irish settlers: the lower middle class builders. Similarly, the City of Boston's Back Bay and Stony Brook sanitary engineering projects and its ag-

FIG. 38. The Mission Church and Back Bay looking north from Parker Hill. The church when new in 1878 (top), and in 1910 with towers added (bottom)

gressive street and water policies made much of the still vacant land suitable for middle class occupancy. Together, the church and the city upgraded the land about this early peripheral immigrant settlement.[23]

During the 1870–1900 period lower middle class families moved into the Tremont street district in two waves. The Irish, then the predominant emergent group of Boston, were the largest element among the newcomers—especially so since there was an established Irish colony in the area. They constituted 44 to 48 percent of the total population, a concentration 10 to 20 percent greater than that in other wards of the three-town suburban area. However, coming with the Irish were lower middle class families of all ethnic backgrounds. A German colony continued for a time, only to be replaced in the 1890's by a wave of Canadians. A mixture of native Americans and minor immigrant groups together comprised the remaining 30 to 40 percent of the population. In the 1890's the beginning Irish settlement on the lowlands around Ruggles street began to be taken over by the next emergent group, the Jews. Throughout the three last decades of the century the whole area served primarily as a "zone of emergence" for lower middle class immigrant families. Between 70 and 80 percent of its population was first and second generation foreign born.[24]

In the postwar building boom which lasted through 1873 cheap row houses filled the vacant lots on the streets off lower Tremont street and up the side of Mission Hill. In the next two decades, especially in the 1885–1895 boom, inexpensive housing of one kind or another covered most of the outer section from Mission Hill to the West Roxbury line. Two new parishes had to be created to supplement the services of the Redemptorists, while their church became one of the most active and important in all Boston. On the rolling hills to the south of Centre street small singles and two families predominated, on the north side of Centre street the three-deckers marched almost uninterrupted from the bottom of the Stony Brook Valley to the very peak of Parker Hill.

These uplands held the potential of some of the handsomest sites and best views of any Boston residential district. However, because the lower middle class had to keep costs to a minimum, and because the general custom of the day dictated narrow frontage lots set on grid streets, all the site potential disappeared beneath rows upon rows of wooden structures all squeezed on small lots. The view became the house opposite; the natural setting was the street, the sidewalk, an occasional street tree, and sometimes a backyard patch of grass or garden.

Not only was this pattern of lower middle class building destructive of nature, it was destructive of itself. It was so finely adapted to the disciplines of the moment that it could not be adjusted to future conditions save through the process of crowding and conversions which only made an already unsatisfactory housing environment even worse. Though the streetcar opened to the lower middle class more land than it had ever before been able to reach, the supply was too little for so large a number of families. These families not only competed with each other, but with industrial and commercial users who were also attracted by the convenience of the inner suburbs.

What one type of user did not purchase, another did. Apartments were built over and behind the stores and three-deckers, and wooden tenements took up the vacant spaces between the factories. This competition for space kept land prices high, the highest of all the sections in the suburbs. Under these conditions each family could afford but little more land than it had controlled in the central city. Cost discipline further required the cheapest known kinds of construction so that most of the new inner suburbs came to be filled with the cheapest acceptable statements of the housing fashions of the day. Once a small area was filled with houses, factories, and stores, there was no way it could respond to a further rise in income or standards among its resident families—they had to move on to fresh land and new neighborhoods.

Similarly, a successful factory frequently required more space, but the pattern of building was so dense that few manufacturers could find room to expand. The Dennison Manufacturing Company in 1880 set up a factory in Roxbury highlands at Vale and Thornton streets. It was an industrial island surrounded by houses. As this stationery company prospered, like the families of Roxbury, it moved further out in the suburbs. The Western Electric Company purchased a square block of land in lower Roxbury[25] but chose instead to build on a much larger parcel in the more distant suburb of Watertown. The once famous Prang's Lithographic Company and the piano factories of the South End and Roxbury chose these locations when their lots were on the edge of the city and land was at once plentiful and moderately convenient to labor and transportation. These companies neither expanded nor moved and after many profitable years they ultimately closed their doors. The process of consolidation and increased scale of business which went on throughout the nineteenth and twentieth centuries left Roxbury with many vacant old industrial buildings unsuited for continued use in their original manner.

By the 1890's Boston's metropolitan region stretched five to ten miles from the downtown. Roxbury no longer offered cheap space on the periphery of the region; instead it was a convenient location for service and distribution industries that wanted to be close to the cheap labor of the inner metropolitan region and handy to the lines of metropolitan distribution. The vacated industrial space of the early years was now filled with users of unskilled labor. As old factories closed or moved, the skilled workers and small businessmen of the district became stranded in their neighborhoods which were but from ten to thirty years old.

Lower middle class neighborhoods were, thus, attacked from sev-

Fig. 39. The old industrial relationship: millowner's house overlooking his mill. House c. 1860, picture 1880

Fig. 40. Stony Brook Valley, workers' houses and mill; houses 1872–3, mill late 1890's

eral directions at once. Changes in housing fashions and transportation brought rapid obsolescence. When these changes occurred, new families of similar income to the original builders could, and did, chose new land and new neighborhoods to live in, rather than taking their places in those already built. Moreover, since land in lower middle class neighborhoods was so densely covered, rising families could only move out if they wished to express their economic progress and gain the housing advantages their new standard of living allowed them. At the same time, the process of industrial change which tended to shift from highly skilled, highly paid employment to ever lower skills, encouraged low paid, low status workers to move into neighborhoods previously dominated by the lower middle class. The cumulative effect of all these forces brought a rapid decline in the social status, personal income level, and housing condition of lower middle class districts. According to contemporary observers by 1900 all of lower Roxbury, then just completed, underwent a shift from a lower middle class to a working class district, and that under the pressure of industrial change and changes in housing preference those families who could afford to leave were rapidly abandoning the area. New low income families, in order to keep rents down, were converting single houses to multiple use, and doubling up in existing multiple dwellings. After but a few years as an acceptable lower middle class neighborhood, lower Roxbury was becoming a slum.[26]

Today the old Roxbury areas of lower middle class building are in an advanced stage of decay and disrepair. Families still occupy the houses because they are inexpensive. All of these structures have not declined equally rapidly, however, a fact which suggests that there may have been more to the rapid decline of the area than the major forces of population and industrial movement reveal. The differing fate of two late nineteenth century housing experiments indicates that in an important sense there were satisfactory and unsatisfactory ways to cheapen a housing fashion.

Off Centre street, at the outer edge of the Tremont street district, just beyond the old shoe factory and the breweries, Robert Treat Paine erected 116 cheap houses in the 1890's. Today, this project is in a neighborhood of well-maintained structures. It was the outgrowth of twenty years' experience in building model houses for the lower middle class. Paine, a descendant of a signer of the Declaration of Independence and a successful corporation lawyer, retired from practice in the 1870's in order to devote himself full time to philanthropic activity. He is justly famous for beginning the Associated Charities movement in Boston. In an age that relied on charity for almost all its social welfare, this movement rendered great service. It brought some order and cooperation among the fragmented charitable organizations of the city.

As a "friendly visitor" in the South End, Paine came upon the contemporary problems of housing, the crowded tenement and the equally crowded row house conversion. He tried in all his charities to ease the burden of the "substantial workingman," the man who despite thrift and middle class aspirations frequently lived in economic jeopardy and tenement squalor. To this end Paine organized unemployment, accident, and sickness benefit groups, educational associations, and a cooperative savings bank. Like most men of his day he felt that individual homeownership was one of the basic elements of satisfactory middle class life. This conclusion led him to experiment with providing safe, sanitary houses at prices the substantial workingman could afford.[27]

In 1874–75, in the inner Tremont street district, Paine built a few brick row houses on Ruggles street. Then, near by, from 1886 to 1890 he undertook a large scale project off Madison Park on Greenwich, Warwick, and Sussex streets. Paine, his brother, and his father-in-law supervised the construction and held the mortgages.[28] They put up Philadelphia style single-family row houses, then the current fashion in philanthropic housing. These were narrow two-story brick structures with about 600 to 800 square feet of floor space, and miniscule pieces of land which provided a rear service alley and enough private space to hold the trash barrels and a baby carriage. To keep land costs down further, narrow alleys were used instead of the standard 40-foot street. The total effect of this subdivision is that of a miniaturized Back Bay executed with all the grace and scale of the old South Boston workingmen's alleys. In support of these mean and unfortunate structures it must be remembered that such houses were then being put up by the thousands in Philadelphia by purchaser-managed cooperative building companies. Furthermore, such houses were then standard stock in trade of English philanthropic builders.[29]

Fig. 41. Philanthropic housing for the "substantial workingman," 1886

Paine's Sussex street houses could be purchased by substantial workingmen for $2,500 apiece, $1,000 in cash and a $1,500 mortgage at 5 percent for five years. Now, seventy years after the event, it is difficult to establish exact price comparisons, but Paine's terms seem to have been usual for suburban houses. The short-term straight mortgage was general. Most mortgagors counted on renewing it several times before finally paying the principal. Indeed, Paine ultimately assigned most of his mortgages to the Boston Safe Deposit and Trust Company. However, the very usualness of the price and terms of Paine's model houses suggests that they were no special bargain. If the substantial workingman were willing in 1886 to sacrifice the convenience of lower Roxbury for a more distant location, he could buy an equally small detached wooden single house with the same capital and get more land and a full sized suburban street. Such limited alternatives led most lower middle class families into renting. They rented old houses, or took parts of the new doubles and three-deckers, moving farther and farther out from Boston as increases in transportation service allowed.

Though Paine's houses and narrow streets may have been suitable for Philadelphia, where there was a long and continuous tradition of row housing, in Boston these buildings had a strong philanthropic air. They were brick and fireproof and had a full set of plumbing facilities, but for all their safety and sanitation they remained mean, cramped row houses built a full decade after the main body of the middle class had ceased building row houses for itself. Like the wooden barracks and tenements of the neighborhood, these houses were suited to the momentary needs and capabilities of their inhabitants—all too suited to them, and not at all suited to their aspirations.

The choice of location was equally suitable and equally unfortunate. In the 1880's much of inner Roxbury was already well established as a lower middle class quarter, so well established that in a few years, as transportation service advanced, large numbers of lower middle class families would leave this inner suburb for more ample surroundings. When they moved, they would leave behind them outmoded and cramped houses which were so small that a mere doubling up of poor families in each structure created conditions similar to those in the North End tenements.

Because Paine had built minimal structures, and built without regard to some of the important middle class aspirations of the day, his houses suffered the fate of all the other homes in the area. For the last forty years they have served as slum dwellings, and, despite Paine's careful construction, they are falling to the ground.

Paine's next undertaking marked a considerable advance in understanding and execution. In this case, instead of building model philanthropic houses, he tried by large-scale planning to improve on ordinary cheap construction. A division of his cooperative bank, the Workingmen's Building Association, served as the central finance and planning agency. This organization purchased several large parcels off Centre street in the outer Tremont street district and laid out its streets and lots in the then advanced method of romantic landscape architecture. This was a cheap project so no handsome yards and vistas resulted, but the streets do follow the contours of the land and are designed to make a traffic cul de sac. By this method more lots with usable space were secured than would have been possible if the current grid street pattern were adopted. Such site planning was just then coming into vogue for expensive subdivisions in Brookline and other parts of greater Boston.

The houses themselves came in several styles of detached frame single and two-family structures. A variety of contemporary ornament was also offered. The house lots were very small but there was a green space to the rear and a little ground and a standard planted suburban street to the front. These houses were more than twice as big as the little row houses of the 1880's and they sold for twice as much. The financing was done by the then still novel amortizing mortgage which reduced the risk both to borrower and lender. The whole suburban "cottagey" effect of this hundred-house subdivision was underlined with street names of "Round Hill" and "Sunnyside."

Had a site been chosen at greater distance from Boston, cheaper land would have allowed a more generous solution, but all developers feared that a distant subdivision might stand vacant for a few years while the main path of building caught up to it. Both Paine and his customers thought in terms of what were then the existing neighborhoods of the city.[30]

Nevertheless Paine's second project was a substantial and permanent contribution. Through the Workingmen's Building Association he succeeded in building at comparable prices a better planned and slightly more landed neighborhood than ordinary private developers were then able to provide. He did this in a place and at a time when the three-decker was the almost universal statement of lower middle class

FIG. 42. Workingmen's Building Association, 1891
model single-family house

building. Today that class has largely deserted this section of Roxbury.
A federal housing project has been required to clean up the 1870
housing of the neighborhood. All around the area, the once popular
three-deckers are in disrepair or a state of partial collapse. Paine's
houses are still kept up, and they are kept up because for sixty years
they have been the best choice of the neighborhood. They have been
the best choice because they were more in keeping with the housing
aspirations of Bostonians than any of the other cheap alternatives of
the 1890's.

The success of Paine's experiment suggests that slum housing is one
of the prices that a society pays for allowing any major amount of its
building to proceed at a level below its common understanding among
the middle class as to what constitutes a satisfactory home environment. Since much late nineteenth century building depended upon
the financial abilities of very restricted family incomes, it could not
have taken any other form than it did. Its cheapness of construction
and meanness of land plan, however, have already brought the des-

struction of neighborhood land and housing values and, so far, two generations of family life set in an environment which for forty years has been incompatible with middle class standards.

Roxbury Highlands

Roxbury highlands was a unique area within the three suburban towns of Roxbury, West Roxbury, and Dorchester. During the last thirty years of the nineteenth century it continued as an area of medium- to high-priced construction while all the other land around it had become centers of lower middle class building. In ethnic and occupational characteristics its population resembled that of the outer suburbs where most of the central and upper segments of the middle class were then building their homes.[31] Its structures and land plans also resembled the outer suburbs except that the closeness of the highlands to Boston made it a profitable location for expensive suburban apartments and some other special rental structures.

The unique characteristics of the highlands delayed its participation in the contemporary outward migration of classes. It was only a delay, not an exemption. Instead of having a large emergent Irish lower middle class living within its boundaries during the years 1870 to 1900, the highlands stayed in the hands of the central segment of the middle class. Then in the twentieth century, the tide of fashion and the movement of classes having passed way beyond it, the highlands became the home first of emergent Jews, and, subsequently, of emergent Negroes.

A combination of three things made Roxbury highlands unique: it was geographically isolated, much of it was built in a form suited to the growing suburban fashion, and it inherited a set of institutions which could, for a time, maintain its small community quality.

In the eighteenth century Roxbury was a farming town which stretched out along the only all-land route to Boston. Cattle and wagons of produce moved along its main roads. Since Roxbury was the place where many roads gathered together to make their way down the Boston Neck, the lower Roxbury village had a minor role as a market town. At this time farms covered the more gradual slopes of the highlands, and a few houses clustered at the margin of the highlands near the town green at Eliot Square and along Dudley and Washington streets.

During the first seventy years of the nineteenth century Roxbury grew in two separate ways. Lowland farms on the Neck, destroyed during the Siege of Boston, were taken up slowly, first for manufacturing and commercial uses, later for homes for Boston's expanding population. Several factors encouraged the industrial development of this area: the water from Stony Brook and Jamaica Pond, the wharves of the South Bay, and the proximity of this part of Roxbury to Boston. By the 1840's lower Roxbury had become one of the several peripheral manufacturing towns which bordered the harbor. Like South Boston, East Boston, Charlestown, and Cambridge, it was partly a residence for those with business in Boston, partly an industrial quarter in its own right.

Roxbury highlands, on the other hand, came to serve a variety of residential uses. The steepness of much of its land kept out industry while the same topography made the highlands land suitable for summer houses and gentlemen's estates. Also, being close to the market center of the town, some of the highlands was taken up with the small houses of the local tradesmen. In the 1840–1873 land boom, the three blocks from Dudley street to Dale street were partly filled with wooden

Fig. 43. Urban styles in Roxbury highlands, marble block, built c. 1870, picture c. 1890

Fig. 44. Cheap wooden imitation of the town row house, 1872. Perhaps such houses were the inspiration for the three-decker

and brick imitations of Boston town houses and detached singles and duplexes. This development was typical of the old peripheral town development where big houses and big lots were mixed in with houses of moderate price. The new construction covered but a small part of the highlands, and all houses were of medium price or better; therefore it did not prejudice the main development of the district.

Beginning in the late eighteenth century men of wealth and fashion built large houses about the hills of Roxbury. During the first thirty-odd years of the nineteenth century, Roxbury highlands and Jamaica Plain were one large district of suburban estates and country houses. The laying of the Boston and Providence Railroad tracks in 1834 and the steady industrial expansion along the Stony Brook Valley cut this area into parts which developed in separate ways. The western Roxbury uplands, a continuation of the Tremont street district, developed as a lower middle class suburb during the 1870–1900 boom. After 1885 another section adjacent to Stony Brook industry, the part of the highlands that lay between Washington street and Columbus avenue, also became an active center of lower middle class building.

The balance of the highlands, roughly a square mile from Washington street to Blue Hill avenue, from Dudley street to Franklin Park, continued to develop in the hands of the central and upper segments of the middle class. This section, unlike any other in the three towns, was both isolated and convenient. The steep hills that rise up from Dudley street caused some isolation. The early roads, Washington street, Warren street, and Blue Hill avenue were laid out to skirt the sharp grades. In this way the main nineteenth century traffic lay at the edges of the district. Further isolation was achieved as an accidental result of the creation of Franklin Park. After 1886 this large park formed the south boundary of the highlands. Streets that cut through the center of the highlands, Walnut avenue and Humboldt avenue, might have ultimately developed heavy traffic loads if the park land had been available for house building. Instead, these streets lead nowhere. Thus, because of the contour if its land and the barrier of Franklin Park, the highlands remained a residential cul de sac.

The historical evolution of Roxbury's institutions also helped to maintain this separateness of the highlands and to isolate it for a time against the main flow of peoples coming to the suburbs. In this case the schools, clubs, and Protestant churches of Roxbury served to continue a middle class Protestant community much in the same way St. Peter's in Dorchester and the Redemptorists on Mission Hill attracted and held for a time special middle class Irish communities. After a while all three neighborhoods shifted into the hands of lower class groups in harmony with the usual patterns of suburban movement.

When families of Protestant immigration speak of "Old Roxbury" they refer to the life of the Roxbury highlands community. On the northeast corner of the district stood the privately managed Roxbury Latin School, the oldest private school in America. Nearby was the home of Dr. Joseph Warren, hero of Bunker Hill and coconspirator of Paul Revere and John Hancock. On the southeast corner stood the town green with its historic Unitarian church; a church founded in 1631–32 which boasted as an early minister, the famous John Eliot, Apostle to the Indians. Between these two outposts, and within the highlands, lay a line of old Revolutionary earthworks, most of the Protestant churches of the town, Roxbury High School, a Lyceum, a private library, and a variety of middle class social clubs.[32]

This array of institutions and symbolic sites was not a conscious arrangement for the defense of the highlands against waves of outward bound immigrants, but owed its placement to the shape of Roxbury's

Fig. 45. First Church (Unitarian), John Eliot Square, Roxbury; church built in 1804, picture c. 1860

ground. The churches and the schools were located on, or adjacent to, the main streets near the point where Roxbury roads gathered together. During the eighteenth and the first half of the nineteenth centuries, the northern boundary of the highlands was the center of town. For this reason, when in 1846 the first Catholic church in town, St. Joseph's, was built it was located in the highlands near Washington and Warren streets. Here it stood in a new subdivision on land that was convenient to all its far flung parishioners.

Many suburban churches were soon needed, and St. Joseph's parish boundaries shrank steadily through the balance of the century. In the late nineteenth century St. Joseph's served middle class Irish families who had moved into the highlands and lower middle class families from adjacent parts of Roxbury. The presence of this church serves as an important reminder of the slight shifts in proportions that mark the different suburban ethnic clusters. Although the highlands was dominated by native American Protestants, in 1880, 38.9 percent of the population of this area were foreign-born and their children; by 1905 the proportion had risen to 57.5 percent. The Irish alone constituted

20 percent of the highlands' population from 1870 to 1900. Such a population mix was characteristic of outer, native American, wards of the city during this period of enormous immigrant absorption.[33]

In the face of such large proportions of newcomers, even such a heavy battery of institutions and symbols as existed in the highlands would have been unable to maintain an effective continuity of tradition if it had not been that most of the tradition of the highlands was central to the whole middle class move to the suburbs.

Before the big suburban rush to Roxbury, prior to its annexation to Boston in 1868, highlands residents dominated the town's affairs. These families enjoyed small community life and actively participated in it. They were vigorous supporters of the rural ideal and romantic landscape planning. One of their number, General Henry A. S. Dearborn, helped to design the Mount Auburn Cemetery in Cambridge, and then persuaded the citizens of Roxbury to build a similar picturesque cemetery as a municipal project. The large Forest Hills Cemetery beyond Franklin Park was the result of this sentiment. The estates of the rich, remnants of which still survive in the southern parts of the highlands, were landscaped in the same manner. Small houses of all sorts bore the ornament and details of similar background. Later, in Boston's two park referenda of 1870 and 1875, the highlands gave favorable majorities that equaled any in the city. Subsequent to the

Fig. 46. Upper middle class suburban single-family houses, picture and houses c. 1890

Fig. 47. Reverend Edward Everett Hale House, 39 Highland street, Roxbury highlands. House c. 1840, now torn down; picture c. 1890

building of the Forest Hills Cemetery, Roxbury itself had no regular policy for the creation of parks. However, the highlands contained the majority of the small squares and parks of the town. These green spaces were the result of gifts and prodding by highlands residents who wished to preserve some of the garden character of the town in the face of the advancing streets of houses.[34]

The orderly management of regular town affairs was another characteristic of Roxbury prior to annexation. Like many middle class suburbs ever since, good schools and a moderate standard of municipal housekeeping were the hallmarks of its government. Social and economic problems went largely untouched. Like most Massachusetts towns, the state-financed dole, supervised by a municipal missionary, represented the limit of the town's welfare measures. The remedy for the bad sanitary condition of most of Roxbury's lowlands required cooperation with Boston in large-scale engineering projects that would have been beyond the means of Roxbury. The Jamaica Pond Aqueduct Company supplied water to parts of town, though most citizens depended upon surface wells. Sewers were few and street paving and lighting modest. However, every year the town laid some new curb, put up a few lights, and from time to time voted new schools as immigration from Boston required. Most residents of the highlands seem to have been contented with the town's rate of municipal progress and during the annexation controversies of the 1850's and 1860's the highlands supplied most of the leaders of antiannexationist policy.[35]

Annexationists claimed the rate of progress was too slow. At this time the conservative elements of the town had the misfortune to face comparison with the city of Boston during one of Boston's most progressive moments. Though Roxbury had a high school and many towns did not, Boston Latin School was better. Though some of Roxbury's main streets had curbs and sidewalks, most of Boston did, and Boston even had some fully paved streets besides. Though Roxbury had a water company, Boston had a great waterworks which served the whole city and could serve all of Roxbury too. So the comparisons went.[36]

Much of the controversy over annexation seems to have been a question of the new middle class settlers in Roxbury demanding new city services to complete their suburban setting. Annexation was also a matter of a new group pressing for power against an old one. The newcomers to Roxbury felt they could join with the middle class of the South End and the other parts of Boston to rule the whole of Boston and Roxbury to their satisfaction. In 1868 they succeeded, and the highlands lost control of Roxbury's affairs. A newcomer to Roxbury and an annexationist, William Gaston, became mayor of Boston in 1871.

Nevertheless, the old schools, churches, and clubs persisted, and they were located in such a way as to serve as centers for the growing middle class suburban neighborhood of Roxbury highlands. They, and their users, remained the dominant force of the neighborhood until the end of the First World War. The old Protestant families only slowly moved away and for many years their places were taken by new families of different ethnic but similar economic standing.

The population profile of Roxbury highlands during the years 1870–1900 remained like that of the outer edge of the suburbs though it was surrounded by lower middle class building. It differed from other suburbs in its higher concentration of professional people and its larger number of households with resident maids. Also, in 1905 the beginning Jewish colony had grown to about 7 percent of the population.

In terms of houses, construction proceeded from the edges of the district toward the center. In general the social status of the land and the size of the houses increased as one approached Franklin Park. On the eastern edge of the district, between Blue Hill avenue and Warren street, the housing boom of the 1880's and 1890's took the form of streets of new single and two-family houses with but few three-deckers. Single and two-family houses in the latest architectural modes gradually took up the vacant land throughout the whole district. Highlands land remained high in status, high in convenience and, therefore, high in price. Large detached houses on smaller lots than those in outer Dorchester or West Roxbury were common to the area. The high price and high social status of land was also reflected in large three-family structures which in their exteriors conformed to the shingle style houses of the neighborhood but did service within as expensive three-deckers. Some apartment houses were also built—three-story apartment row houses, and tall apartment hotels. These apartment houses crowded the land and destroyed its garden effect just as the three-deckers did elsewhere. However, they did not take a major part of the land until after the First World War. In the 1920's large

FIG. 48. High-priced multiple housing: suburban apartment hotel, Roxbury highlands. Hotel built 1884, picture c. 1890

Fig. 49. Expensive three-deckers, Roxbury highlands. Houses and picture c. 1890

numbers of apartments were built for Jewish families coming into the district.

Throughout the nineteenth century the highlands remained as much a garden suburb as any large section of the three towns of Roxbury, West Roxbury, and Dorchester. To most middle class families of the 1870–1900 era its land arrangements were eminently satisfactory. In addition to its housing and land plan, the highlands possessed the advantages of a homogeneous middle class community located close to Boston. The 1891 rental survey conducted by the state of Massachusetts further attests to the degree of satisfaction of highlands residents. Here was located more than half the premium rental space of the three towns. The rented suites and houses were not only larger than elsewhere but the price per room was higher. Almost half the rental units in the highlands went at the premium rates.[37]

The special conditions of social movement and house building in Roxbury highlands during the 1870–1900 period were but one of the eddies in the general flow of middle class Bostonians out from the center of the city to vacant suburban land. The history of the highlands community is much the same as that of the central middle class cluster about St. Peter's parish of inner Dorchester, or the lower middle class Irish cluster about the Redemptorist Church. There were many such suburban eddies, and they formed and dissolved with the general outward flow of population.

Today, although there is one dynamic middle class group residing in the area, the Negroes, Roxbury—the highlands, the Tremont street district, the lower town—is for the most part a run-down area. Physical deterioration has been especially severe in the old districts of lower middle class building. The churches, the stores, the parks, and the schools, all once active, prosperous, and well kept, are now either struggling along in the old ways or are engaged in the difficult process of adapting themselves to the service of the modern urban poor. It is a hard task at best, for the churches are either too large, of the wrong denomination, or in the wrong place. The schools designed to teach candidates for Boston Latin and English high schools now face a generation of children many of whom will never complete high school. Most students are destined to enter the large pool of Boston's unskilled labor force. Parks and stores share the common problems of the wrong locations, antique plant, and the need for new marketing modes to service a different kind of customer.

Most of the problems of Roxbury today are not primarily housing problems, but the problems of urban society as a whole. The houses of Roxbury are but the vestiges of an earlier, rapidly changing society which built to the measure of the moment and then left its remains for others to use as best they could.

CHAPTER SIX

REGULATION WITHOUT LAWS

THE STRIKING uniformity of land plans and architecture which characterized late-nineteenth-century suburbs was, in large measure, the product of a building process which rested in the hands of thousands of small agents. In the three towns of Roxbury, West Roxbury, and Dorchester during the thirty years from 1872 to 1901, nine thousand different people made separate decisions to build houses. Precisely because small contractors and individual homeowners made the construction decisions, force of circumstances possessed great power to delimit their field of choice. Somewhat paradoxically, from the extreme individualization of agency in the building process came great uniformity of behavior, a kind of regulation without laws.

Two historical conditions contributed to the widespread division of agency: the short supply of capital and the availability of large quantities of easily developed land at the edge of the old city of Boston.

One of the principal accomplishments of nineteenth-century America was to settle and industrialize a continent. This effort consumed enormous quantities of capital; railroads, farms, factories, and cities had to be built from nothing. Western land companies, railroads, and oil, mining, and manufacturing companies—undertakings which required wholesale purchases and large-scale operations for successful development—were promoted and financed by international syndicates of London, Paris, and New York businessmen. The foreign funds supplied to large American enterprises allowed the nation to tie up money at a faster rate than it could generate fresh capital for long-term investment.

With a voracious domestic demand for capital American banks could best operate with safety and profit by lending money to wholesalers, traders, and other short-term users. When long-term commitments became the basis for banking the results were often disastrous.[1] Boston was a center of American finance and better supplied with capital than most regions. Also, since 1834 Massachusetts had established a number of mutual savings banks that served as a useful means of gathering small savings and pooling them for mortgage investment. National conditions, however, controlled the Boston money market, and the savings banks could finance but a small fraction of the total investment needed to house the population of a rapidly growing metropolis. In the absence of widespread bank participation, thousands of private investors made up the mortgage market. They lent money to homeowners and builders in small quantities for terms of six months to ten years.

The unsettled conditions of contemporary large capital markets to some extent drove small investors into the mortgage field. The behavior of the New York Stock Exchange during the last three decades of the nineteenth century offered unusual opportunities to the Drews and the Vanderbilts, but it led many men with only a few thousand dollars of free capital to look elsewhere for safe investment. In a period marked by unregulated stock and bond prospectuses, insurance frauds, bank failures, and financial jobbery of all kinds, investment in local real estate had many advantages for those whose only method of capital accumulation was hard work and saving. Bonds and stocks of well-established railroads and utilities and a few state and municipal bonds might attract some, and in Massachusetts savings bank deposits were always a convenient source of income, but suburban real estate offered advantages these investments could not match.[2]

Suburban real estate provided an open, readily accessible market in which capital could be invested in moderate quantities. In these days before automobiles and the widespread use of the telephone, downtown Boston was the location of the metropolitan real estate market, and in almost any office building there a prospective investor or home buyer could find a wide range of mortgage and land offerings. The daily newspapers carried columns of advertisements by Boston dealers for all kinds of metropolitan properties and investments. Unlike today, when suburban dealers are located apart from the central city dealers, and each town has its own bank and own real estate specialists, in the nineteenth century the mortgage agents and sellers of land and houses were clustered together. This centrality made mortgage trading easy and thereby kept the market more liquid and flexible than it might have been had investors been required to restrict themselves to local opportunities.[3]

Small investors could easily acquire a fairly expert knowledge about the part of the metropolitan area in which they lived. With this expertise they might reasonably expect to reap part of the harvest of capital gain inherent in the rapid expansion of the city. This degree of certainty of appreciation was an element lacking in the more daring stock investment. For those interested in a home of their own or rental investments, one or two thousand dollars was the minimum capital requirement. Mortgagees could risk as little as five hundred dollars for as short a term as six months.

To some extent the mortgages themselves were adapted to the needs of an unregulated market of small investors. By today's standards the terms were short, and the proportion of the loan to the total value of the property was smaller. Mortgages granted by speculative builders while development was in progress normally ran from one to three years. The individual landowner putting up his own house often worked on longer terms, from three to eight years. Research in contemporary records failed to reveal a mortgage of more than ten years.

The common practice of the first and second mortgage may also have been a custom supported by the nature of a market of small investors. The total of the first and second mortgages generally amounted to no more than 50 percent of the value of the property. The first mortgage, which took 30 to 40 percent of the value, was protected by its legal right to satisfaction prior to other debts. The second mortgage, about 10 to 15 percent of the total value, generally was granted only after much of the work on the house had been completed. Second mortgage holders, taking a greater risk due to their subordinate standing, often received ½ to 1 percent more interest, and always lent for six-month to three-year terms. By this device of two mortgages the market divided itself into two groups: the speculative investors and the conservatives. Second mortgage specialists were generally real estate professionals, men who were prepared to take over a failing project, if necessary, in order to protect their investment.[4]

Curiously enough, the amortizing mortgage was a rarity in the period. An amortizing mortgage is paid by successive installments of principal and interest and thereby protects mortgagees against insolvency of mortgagors. Only an occasional private investor and the cooperative banks used this form of loan. Overwhelmingly mortgages were written for semiannual interest payments of 5 to 6 percent with a lump sum repayment of principal at the end of the term. The failure of the market to use a known device for its own protection can only be explained by the traditionalism of real estate practices and the general optimism of the period.[5]

The optimism of the day found its way into real estate via the notion of improvement. According to this doctrine, if a man put up a house on a vacant lot he thereby improved his property and the property of his neighbors. By this act he encouraged others to build. Thus, in a few years he could expect his property to be worth more than when the mortgage was first let. His mortgagee could then renew the mortgage with greater safety than when he first advanced the money. The borrower, in turn, felt confident that if he were unable to pay at the end of the term other lenders would come forward to advance him the needed capital.

The rapid growth of the metropolis lent some truth to this line of reasoning. The sudden shifts in building patterns within the various suburban areas, however, did not automatically raise all the neighboring values. For example, as was shown in the previous chapter, a rash of lower middle class three-deckers could destroy much of the future value of a neighborhood of medium-priced singles.

Moreover, business optimism with its accompanying satisfaction with short-term mortgages exposed both the borrower and the lender to unnecessary risks. Thousands of homeowners depended on the renewal of their mortgages at close to the full amount. In hard times this system worked considerable hardship on those who found themselves unable to renew. There were disadvantages for the lender, too, since the renewal system tended to intensify panics and widen swings in building activity.

The conditions of the mortgage market affected tenure patterns in the suburbs. Though ownership of a single-family home was one of the goals of suburban life, in 1900 only 25 percent of the families living in the suburbs owned their own homes. The rest, either through lack of the required capital or fear of the risks involved, chose to rent. Likewise, multiple structures were popular; indeed, in the same year 40 percent of the houses in Dorchester, Roxbury, and West Roxbury were two- and three-family or large multiple structures.[6]

Nevertheless, despite these limitations, in the thirty years studied only the Depression of 1873–1878 was severe enough to stop the flow of suburban building. For the rest of the time, though an individual builder might make a mistake and go bankrupt, the metropolis rushed on in triumph, the rate of expansion itself providing short-term safety of investment.

Metropolitan Boston's mortgage market was a market of thousands of individuals organized around the many downtown real estate men and mortgage brokers who through personal contact and solicitation linked small private accumulations of capital to the task of building houses. In an important sense, building practices in the late nineteenth century were the means whereby the metropolis financed its own development.[7] The successive stages of building, from the original subdivision to the final occupancy by resident families, engaged more and more small units of capital until at the end of the process hundreds of people may have joined together to develop what was formerly one man's thirty-acre farm.

The ordinary course of building proceeded by two major steps: first, the subdivision and preliminary land development; second, the purchase of lots and construction of houses.[8] At the outset a speculator purchased a large vacant plot. Such a parcel might vary from eight to forty acres, that is, from one to six blocks in size, depending upon previous street layouts and subdivisions. The speculator paid for this land either entirely with cash, or partly with cash and partly with a mortgage. The advantage to full cash payment lay in the subsequent opportunity for the speculator to limit his liability by the use of a legal fiction. Often, immediately after purchase, the speculator sold his land to a straw, a *pro forma* purchaser. By this procedure, he would be protected against personal liability.[9]

Whether or not the device of the straw was used the main task of the speculator was to cut up the land into house lots, begin construction of streets, and find purchasers for the land. Only rarely did the speculators of this era follow the modern practice of purchasing land, setting out streets, and building houses in order to sell a finished land-house unit to the ultimate consumer. Such a process required the tying up of more capital than most could command.

The speculator usually mortgaged his land in order to finance the construction of streets. The City of Boston required a rough graded street before it would undertake to supply its water and sewer services, set curbs, put up lights, and formally accept the street for permanent municipal maintenance. However, up until 1891 and the creation of the Board of Survey, subdividers enjoyed almost complete freedom in the choice of location and grades for their streets.[10]

After beginning street construction the speculator sought three kinds of customers: builders who would purchase a few lots and put up houses on their own account, real estate dealers who would take several lots and would find builders and family purchasers for them, and individuals who wanted to speculate in a suburban parcel or purchase a lot for their own home. These customers were found either by auctions or by solicitation. The public auction of the lots was the simplest and quickest procedure. It was effective for subdivisions located in popular, partially developed neighborhoods. In more distant or less popular areas the speculator had to act as salesman for his own projects.

Toward the end of the century there was a marked increase in the degree of control that subdividers tried to exercise over their purchasers. The use of covenants, which had formerly accompanied Boston's large-scale land development schemes, now came into general suburban use. These covenants restricted purchasers to single-family houses, or forbade three-family or larger multiple structures. The minimum costs of houses to be erected were often established. Factories, saloons, and livery stables were almost always targets of residential covenants. Builders and individual purchasers sometimes agreed to put up a house within a year or two on pain of forfeiting their land. Set back and side yard lines limiting the placement of houses to certain positions on the lot, restrictions against fences or limits on their height, and rules governing the number and size of collateral structures were general. All these legal restrictions were directed toward the goal of rapid and uniform development of the subdivision.

As experience with suburbs increased it was found that middle class customers preferred uniform neighborhoods to mixed ones. In the absence of modern zoning, or one-man control of large-scale developments, speculators used covenants of 15–25 years duration to ensure homogeneity of structures and land use. There is no evidence, however, of the use of covenants against any racial, religious, or national group.[11]

At the time when the individual lots began to change hands the subdivision frequently disappeared into a legal miasma of considerable complexity. The speculator's mortgage hovered over the whole subdivision. It generally allowed for partial extinguishment as each lot was sold. Thus, when a builder bought "numbers 27–36" these lots would be removed from the speculator's mortgage after he had paid some agreed fraction of his debt to his mortgagee. The speculator did not often receive cash from the builder, however, but took a down payment and a mortgage. At this point he frequently turned his attention to locating customers for the builder's first mortgages. As the work progressed on a house or two the builder sought second mortgages to finance their completion. At the time of sale of a house and lot to the ultimate purchaser the property was cleared of its former mortgages and refinanced in the name of the new owner.

The combined transactions of the speculator, the real estate dealers, the mortgage holders, the builders, and the homeowners could, in a few years time, fill pages of the county records. Today, with banks providing large sums, such changing of hands and multiplication of small mortgages is unnecessary. The subdivider works with one large flexible mortgage which covers his costs from the moment of purchase through the completion of the houses to the final sale of the land-house units.

In a period short of capital, however, the system of divided agency and successive mortgages had the advantage of gathering ever new sources of money. In the building of a typical house five persons would contribute capital in the time between the division of the land and the final sale of the house and lot to its occupant. For example, in the case of a $4,000 house-lot unit, two groups contributed a total of about $3,440 exclusive of interest payments: the land speculator and his mortgagee, $440; the builder and his mortgagees, $3,000. The land speculator, in this hypothetical case, would pay $200 for the land. In the expectation that he could sell it for $600 he would borrow $240 (40 percent of the sales price) to pay for the costs of grading the adjacent street, and bringing in the utilities. A builder then purchased the lot for $600 cash and added $1,000 of his own to pay for the materials and labor necessary to put up the house. He also borrowed from a first mortgage lender $1,600 (40 percent of the sales price) to raise money to meet his expenses. As the house neared completion he would borrow $400 more (10 percent of the sales price) from a second mortgage lender. When the house was complete the builder would have invested $1,600 of his own money, the first mortgage lender $1,600, the second mortgage lender $400. When the house and lot were sold to the final purchaser the builder pocketed a $400 profit. If a builder erected more than one house in a year his work often involved several different first and second mortgage lenders. Today a subdivision of 200 houses requires the decision of a banker and a speculator; in the late nineteenth century such a development could easily generate more agents than houses.

The second historical condition which contributed to the diffusion of agency in metropolitan building was the availability of easily developed land beyond the edge of the old central city. The Back Bay project, begun in the 1860's, was the last of the large-scale undertakings of the nineteenth century. Big syndicates had developed much of Boston's residential land; syndicates were responsible for the Beacon Hill, Pemberton Hill, North Cove, and South End projects. To fill marshes and to level hills, to do all the work necessary to make land fit for house building, required large-scale organization. Even subdivisions in peripheral towns like South Boston and East Boston were financed in this way because they needed bridges, ferries, and extensive public works before purchasers could be lured out to the property. The uniqueness of the Back Bay project came from its size, which was so great as to require state finance for its execution.

Given such a tradition, the development of residential land in the three towns might have remained in the hands of big syndicates had not the City of Boston undertaken its large-scale street and sanitation program. After annexation in the 1870's the city connected the existing villages into one integrated street and sanitary system. With this construction, and the new horsecar service, acres of land were thrown open to small-scale development. Along the old country roads outside Boston there were acres of uplands suited to immediate homebuilding.

The small developer and individual purchaser was further favored by the existing patterns of suburban land tenure. The number of titles to be assembled by promoters in the South Boston, East Boston, East Cambridge, and Beacon Hill projects were few. The marshlands on the edge of Boston were frequently held by many individuals, but the need for common action against tidal flooding drove owners into agreement. In the new suburbs the land was held in thousands of parcels, most in some form of satisfactory use; as a result nothing forced landowners into joint action. Truck and dairy farmers, railroad commuters, and estate owners held much of the land. Frequently, subdividers in the suburbs were these very parties, or village families who owned a field outside of town. Even if big syndicates had been active in the suburbs such conditions of tenure would have made it difficult to assemble tracts which would be both large and convenient to transportation and city services.[12]

There was a notable exception to the general shift to small operations which took place in the streetcar era: the planning and layout of Beacon street in Brookline. In 1886 Henry M. Whitney and his associates in the West End Land Company bought farms along what was then a popular country drive. With the aid of the town of Brookline they made Beacon street into a model French boulevard. Simultaneously they formed the West End Street Railway to bring customers to their property. The operation was a success and in the ensuing decade the land sold well. However, the rarity of this kind of enterprise suggests that small-scale development might have been equally profitable.[13]

It is important to remember that Boston's post–Civil War shift to small-scale operations concerned land organization only. Even the best financed projects of the earlier era rarely undertook to build any houses for their customers. To do so would have required more capital than they could muster. The South End, Back Bay, East Boston, and other syndicates prepared lots for sale. The capital for houses had to be provided by the individual purchaser and his mortgagee.

Because of the nature of the mortgage market and the divided tenure of suburban land the building of the metropolis went forward with thousands of small-scale operations. This method of constructing a city had many important consequences for the metropolitan environment. Briefly, the final agent of metropolitan construction was the individual builder. Because he was an individual capitalist working on an extremely small scale and with only limited resources his area of concern and range of responsibility could not help but be proportionately small. The builder's choices were very limited; they were further limited by his lack of experience with cities and his lack of professional training. The builder, often engaged in a race with interest charges, sought safety in speed of production and fast turnover. He sought safety by dividing land and building houses in the popular style of the moment. Out of the extreme division of agency came extreme discipline of the agents by forces beyond their control. Despite 9,000 separate builders, only one land plan and a few basic house

Fig. 50. Contractors' building with Owen Nawn's shop, Roxbury; picture, 1894

styles dominated the new metropolitan suburbs of Roxbury, West Roxbury, and Dorchester. A more detailed examination of the background and circumstances of the builders will illustrate the consequences of this method of city building.

The Home Builders

In order to identify individual action within so populous a field as 9,000 suburban landowners, small numbers must be selected to speak for the whole. Accordingly, a representative group of 361 names, drawn at random from the whole thirty-year list, was chosen for summary examination. A second group was made up of the 122 most active landowners, men who built twenty or more houses on their own property* during the years 1872–1901. By combining the summary facts about the representative group of 361, with detailed information

---

* The meager requirement necessary to enter the ranks of the most active further indicates the divided quality of suburban residential construction. The most active landowner put up 328 houses, the next two big builders put up 174 and 132 houses apiece. Most of the group erected between 20 and 40 houses. Taken together the group as a whole contributed 5,350 houses, or 23 percent of all the new dwellings in the three towns.

of the lives of the most active group of 122, a good deal can be inferred about the background, conditions, and motives of the whole body of 9,000 suburban builders.

Except for a few of the most active landowners the men who made the decisions to build were all local middle class amateurs. In addition, perhaps a majority of the houses were erected by men with no prior experience with cities, men who had come to Boston from small New England and Canadian towns.[14]

By definition, all suburban builders were middle class. In Boston the system of long-term ground rents was not used in residential building. The title to the land and its structure was not separated as was frequently the case in Pennsylvania or England. Thus, the owner of the land at the time of application for a building permit had to have sufficient capital to finance the final land-house combination. In the last third of the nineteenth century the financial minimum for new-home ownership hovered around $2,000-$4,000. In other words, to be a suburban builder one had to have accumulated about $1,000-$2,000 cash, and have sufficient standing to get mortgage credit in an equal amount.

The typical builder used his knowledge as a local resident for the selection of his property. He built on land near his own house. In both the representative group and the group of active landowners, between 70 and 80 percent of those of known addresses lived in the three towns of Roxbury, West Roxbury, and Dorchester when they applied for building permits. Thirty-five to 40 percent of both groups lived within two blocks of the houses they put up. Just as the metropolis financed itself so the suburb was built by the suburbanites.

Such a large measure of local participation indicates a considerable harmony of taste among buyers and sellers. In the suburbs, at least, outsiders did not force cheap construction upon incoming families. In lower Roxbury a local political boss, Timothy Connolly, put up cheap brick three-family row housing for Irish tenants. Connolly's houses furnished cramped quarters with little light and air. However, the builder lived in one himself, and he must have felt that what was good enough for him was good enough for his tenants. Such a situation was the rule throughout the three towns. Whatever was good or bad about the building in a neighborhood was largely the product of decisions made by small investors who lived there or nearby.

Three motives seem to have been behind the decisions of most

Fig. 51. Timothy Connolly's 1894 minimum housing. Adjacent houses have been torn down

landowners: a man built a new house for himself or his family, or he built to invest his money as a neighborhood landlord, or he built hoping to make a profit by offering a house or two for sale. Owing to the popularity of two- and three-family houses these motives could often be combined in a single structure. Forty percent of the representative sample built for their own use as well as the use of others and the proportion of active landowners combining business with family residence was about the same.

Sixty percent of all the suburban landowners taking out building permits put up an average of only 1.15 dwellings during the thirty years studied. The next largest group of landowners (17.5 percent) put up an average of 3.87 dwellings. Thus, house building was not a major occupational concern for 77.5 percent of all the landowners. Together this group built 15,225 dwellings, or 71.5 percent of all the new residential structures of Roxbury, West Roxbury, and Dorchester during the years 1872–1901.

Because of the amateur nature of suburban building occupational distinctions were not very significant. As might be expected, the building trades dominated the group of the most active landowners—some

71.3 percent of these were in construction or real estate. In the representative group the building trades and real estate men were also dominant, contributing 39.3 percent of the whole group's structures. However, the remainder of the list reads like a catalogue of the occupations then open to Boston's middle class: lawyers, grocers, clerks, piano makers, pressmen. Together these professionals, businessmen, and skilled artisans contributed 32.4 percent of the representative sample's dwellings. Persons of unknown occupation made up the balance of 28.3 percent.

Among those whose background could be traced, the overwhelming proportion of the most active landowners came from the country, not from cities. This strong rural background may well have had an effect upon the architecture of the city itself. As opposed to the formal architecture of the preceding period, which was a conscious adaptation of London and Paris styles, the new streetcar suburbs looked like an enormous proliferation of the small town. This new appearance was largely the product of middle class Bostonians' interest in the rural ideal, but the small town look may also have gathered further popularity from being the work of men from the country.

The Maritime Provinces of Canada provided as many of the most active landowners as did Greater Boston, and most of the rest came from the small towns of Massachusetts, Maine, New Hampshire, and Vermont. A common phrase of the day used to describe suburban contractors was, "Nova Scotia hatchet and saw men." The phrase covers in a rough and ready way the whole group of most active landowners.

The depressed condition of New England and Maritime farms during the last half of the century was the ultimate cause of the large rural migration to Boston. The concentration of these immigrants in the building trades is, however, harder to explain. A love of outdoor work and a youthful training in forest trades and farm carpentry probably led so many country boys to choose the construction industry. Unlike the Irish peasant, who was potentially his chief competitor, a farm boy arriving in Boston spoke English with an accent most employers and customers enjoyed. Though he was hardly an accomplished carpenter, he was at least familiar with the tools and knew something of wooden frame construction.

These initial advantages and partial skills probably accounted for the prevalence of men of rural background in suburban building.

Though there is no way of knowing the origin of all the suburban landowners, it seems reasonable to assume that among those who worked in the building trades the rural background was the ranking one, as it was among the small group of most active landowners.

This summary information about the background and activities of suburban builders tells much about the rationale of construction in this era. The typical agent for the construction of the major residential sections of the metropolis was a middle class amateur who made a few local investments and who often as not had spent his youth on a farm or in some small New England or Maritime town. Such a man was well matched to the major characteristics of suburban building.

Because a landowner considering a new house was a local investor he could know the status value of the land he would purchase. Because he was a middle class man he would respect the classification of people by income. Some contemporaries lamented that more and more homeowners considered houses as products to be bought and sold like so much cloth, not as permanent family homesteads.[15] There may well have been an increase in the commercial attitude toward houses, as there was an increase in the commercial attitude toward much else in late-nineteenth-century America. However, for a society like Boston's, which was beset by ethnic tensions, the dollar valuation of people served a useful equalitarian function. It opened new suburban neighborhoods to all comers with sufficient cash to meet the price.

Because the suburban builder was an amateur he was a willing follower of popular housing fashions. Without any formal training in architecture or subdivision, and hard pressed by lack of capital, he sought safety by repeating the popular. Several convenient sources of information guided landowners' choices. The new houses in his vicinity were probably the most instructive and influential models. A completed building was easier to comprehend than plans or articles, and a finished structure carried the sanction of being a proved risk. It stood as tangible evidence of a neighbor's successful solution to an investment problem similar to the one facing the man contemplating new construction.

In addition to personal observation, landowners used local contractors' sketches of houses recently built and the stock plans of builders' manuals. Architects were not commonly the designers of medium-priced housing in the late nineteenth century. Trained architects were few, and only the rich were in the habit of employing them. Most families regarded the architect's fee as an unnecessary extra expense. The carpenters and builders themselves or self-taught draftsmen in contracting or real estate offices drew most of the plans for suburban houses.

Finally, the popular middle class magazines like *Godey's* and *Scribner's* carried a steady stream of articles on architecture and interior decoration. These articles reflected the interest of their readers in the affairs of homeownership and guided aspiring middle class families who faced house construction for the first time.

Given such sources of information, most of the work of suburban landowners displayed some individuality in choice of ornament and detail but was repetitive in basic house and lot plan. Amateur investors possessed neither the skill nor the motivation to engage in any orderly rethinking of how a house should be adapted to the new conditions of suburban family life. Instead styles set by architects of the rich descended rapidly through the various levels of middle class building. Men copied the fashions of the wealthy regardless of whether designs appropriate to Newport estates would be satisfactory to suburban families when executed at one-tenth their original scale.[16]

Italian and mansard details gave way in the 1870's to Queen Anne and shingle style adaptations of Newport houses. These in turn were abandoned in the 1890's for colonial ornament. Within the limits of trends in style, the selection of millwork and the placing of porches, bays, and towers was left to the home builder's personal choice. The modern observer is at first bewildered by the variety of combinations attempted. After a tour of a few blocks, however, the essential sameness of the underlying house and land plans becomes apparent.

Between 1870 and 1900 middle class housing underwent but few changes. The detached frame house replaced row housing after 1873. The single-family wooden house became the suburban trade mark and all other kinds of structures copied its appearance. The popularity of the single brought by imitation the horizontal division of two- and three-family houses. Double houses were popular before the Civil War. In these houses the two suites stood side by side, joined by a party wall. After 1873 landlord and tenant lived one above the other and frequently shared a common first-floor entrance. The only other major change in the basic form of houses came in the 1890's

FIG. 52. Double house, c. 1840–1850

when continued increases in the quantities of land and the return to colonial styles brought a shift from predominance of long narrow plans to predominance of square floor plans.

Despite these changes the 9,000 suburban builders active from 1872–1901 built in but one basic form: front-facing detached structures which were centered on long narrow lots and set in rows within a pattern of grid streets. Much of this uniform response by thousands of independent agents came from the common situation they all faced in the arrangement of their land.

THE GRID STREET AND FRONTAGE LOT

From 1870 to 1900 the grid street and frontage lot system was the land plan that underlay almost all the building in the three towns of Roxbury, West Roxbury, and Dorchester. It was a simple device which had been used in Europe off and on since Roman times. A series of streets laid out in two parallels, one tier of parallels at right angles to the other, forms a grid. Land between streets so arranged takes the shape of a series of regular rectangular blocks. If the land within these blocks is divided down the middle every lot within the block becomes a frontage lot—a lot which faces directly on at least one street.

The grid system had many advantages, one of the most important in America being its simple repetitive geometry which made it an easy method for surveying wilderness land. In 1787 the grid system was undertaken on a continental scale by the enactment of the Northwest Land Ordinance. Thousands of western towns owe their grid arrangement to this program initially adopted to meet the requirements of government surveyors.

Much of New England had been settled before the application of the federal policy, however, and its wilderness land lay outside the federal domain. In many of its cities and towns land had been traded for 150 years prior to the Northwest Ordinance. Original village plans

Fig. 53. The narrow mansard house, c. 1878; picture c. 1880

Fig. 54. The square house, Colonial Revival, 1898

had long since been outgrown and in places of dense settlement the houses and lots took forms demanded by geographical requirements and historical events. Here the grid street and frontage lot system came into extensive use because it was suited to nineteenth-century urban conditions. This method of land division, first introduced by speculators in imitation of current European fashions, became popular because it could be adapted to meet a variety of market situations, because it minimized the cost of new streets and utilities, and because it maintained established standards for land and house orientation.

For men of wealth in 1800, Boston looked too much like a country town. Shops and houses crowded narrow crooked streets while many of the houses of the rich, just because they were set on ample garden lots, looked like country houses strung along a village road. With the growing wealth and refinement of manners, Bostonians in the early nineteenth century took up the town house fashion of Georgian London, and its companion grid street system of subdivision.

The new style depended upon an orderly integration of the street and its houses. The block was made up of parallel rows of narrow attached houses, each row facing a street. In medium and high-priced developments the service alley and backyards formed a courtyard behind the houses, but in cheap rows the houses were backed up to each other so that the only light and air came from the street side. To guard against fire, and to further the urban look, the houses were brick and sometimes stone. In expensive projects little parks of various shapes broke the monotony of long straight streets. Uniform building lines and heights were customary and rows of uniform façades frequent.

This popular system of land division and architecture produced new residential streets that looked orderly, prosperous, and citified. The regular streets and paved sidewalks flanked by continuous bands of brick construction gave visible testimony to the importance of the city and the cultivated taste of its inhabitants. For eighty years, from Bulfinch's Crescent of 1793 through the Depression of 1873, row houses and grid streets were Boston's model form of building. The South End and Back Bay are the largest areas constructed from these plans, but from about 1820 on patches of similar construction dotted

FIG. 55. London style row houses of Boston's South End. Union Park street; laid out in 1851

the whole of the old pedestrian city and its peripheral towns of Roxbury, Cambridge, Charlestown, and East and South Boston. Even where cheap wooden detached houses dominated, as in East and South Boston, the grid street and frontage lot plan was used to divide the land.

Around the late 1860's the balance of forces that governed styles of building shifted once more, this time against the city. Continued and accelerated industrialization and immigration brought a mounting interest in the rural ideal among middle class city dwellers. The street railroad provided the land necessary for new detached housing styles. The change in architecture, however, was more pronounced than the change in land planning. Although London and Paris row house styles were abandoned by the middle class after 1873, both the narrow frontage lot and the grid street were carried out to the suburbs. The expansion of the frontage lot to twice and three times its former area constituted the principal change in land planning.

Middle class Bostonians brought to the suburban situation standards first established by the grid street and frontage lot, standards which they had grown to regard as necessary minima for a satisfactory residential environment. They demanded equal access to a neat graded street, equal light and air, and a somewhat uniform facade for the entire street. These requirements remained constant elements for middle class builders and buyers throughout the century. The back alley houses of eighteenth-century Boston, the alleys of South Boston, and the brand new tenement alleys of the West and North End were unacceptable to suburbanites.

From 1870 to 1900, except for a few lower middle class units built where traffic arteries made land prices high, none of the houses in Roxbury, West Roxbury, and Dorchester were built on any but frontage lots facing full-sized streets. Where new streets were laid the forty-foot grid street was almost universal. Though detached houses now became the rule the continued use of uniform building lines and the habit of centering houses with equal sideyards gave all residents on a street a rough equality of light, air, and access. Further, the movement of building by income waves gave most streets for short periods, and many streets for long periods, a uniformity in building costs. This uniformity created a homogeneous statement of social and economic status despite great variety of ornament. In this way the continuation of popular standards first learned in the pre–Civil War

Fig. 56. Public Alley no. 15, West End before demolition.
Wooden houses c. 1840–1850. Original siding clapboards

period produced the well-known suburban street: rows of detached
houses with carefully tended lawns and shrubs in front, all ranged
along a neat planted and finished street.[17]

The achievement of these popular minimum standards did not,
however, require the use of the grid street and frontage lot. The division of land into irregular lots which followed the contours of the site
and the use of the winding path of the romantic park could have
achieved the same results, as twentieth century subdividers later
proved. The grid street and frontage lot system persisted throughout
the nineteenth century because it both met the minimum requirements
of middle class house buyers and solved the problems of small-scale
subdividers and builders.

The suburban developer of the late nineteenth century had to take
his land as he found it. He possessed little capital for the preparation

of lots. Before the Civil War, in the days of the pedestrian city, when land was expensive, large syndicates had undertaken extensive alteration of sites. The plenty of inexpensive land available to the streetcar city threw land speculation open to thousands of small investors whose profit lay in cutting up land that needed little preliminary investment.

The relative cheapness of suburban land, however, was offset by a rise in the cost of streets. The late nineteenth century street included both the surface of gravel, granite curbs, and brick sidewalks and the water, gas, and sewer lines. Toward the end of the century it also included electric and telephone lines. The position of the land vis-à-vis these new sanitary and power services was of vital concern to the subdivider.[18]

Much of the vacant land lay in long strips at right angles to the old country roads. This pattern was the result of two historical forces. In the two centuries when Dorchester, Roxbury, and West Roxbury were predominantly farming communities roads constituted a heavy community expense, and the towns built as few as possible. Second, farmers could till a narrow rectangular field more easily than a square one since the long rectangle required fewer arduous turns of plows, cultivators, and wagons. As a result of these two circumstances land-trading prior to the residential development of the three towns tended to divide parcels into long strips oriented with narrow frontages toward the scarce and expensive roads.

When the city of Boston annexed the three towns it ran its water and sewer mains down the established country roads. Street railway, gas, electric, and telephone companies all followed the same practice since these old arteries connected the most existing houses. This placement of services by itself exerted a strong tendency for the development of land at right angles to the main traffic arteries. A subdivider who purchased a farm field beside one of these roads could most cheaply connect all the utilities by running a street or two down the length of his land.

Though charges for utilities varied considerably throughout the 1870 to 1900 period, the owner of the new land to be served always paid a substantial proportion of the cost of installation. Thus, any device that reduced the number of feet of curb, pipe, and paving would give a direct saving to the developer and thereby increase his chance for profit when he resold his land for house lots.

The developers' marketing situation transformed this tendency toward rectangular land division into an imperative for the use of street grids and narrow frontage lots. Since middle class Bostonians demanded more or less equal access to a full street, developers were barred from using the more land-conserving technique of widely separated main streets with interior lots served by small alleys. Given this limitation, a subdivider could maximize his house lot area and minimize his street surface area by using the regular grid street and frontage lot system. In a typical subdivision of this style the street consumed about one quarter of the land area. In cases where the subdivider wanted to maximize his lot sizes, the longer he could make his rectangular blocks the better, because as the number of cross streets increased so did the proportion of land taken up by street surface. In central Dorchester, where lot sizes were fairly generous and subdividers could purchase large farm fields, the blocks are longer than in old residential sections where vacant land came on the market in smaller parcels.

In a small parcel a developer often put in cross streets in order to increase the number of frontage lots for sale even though he had thereby to sacrifice more of his total lot area. The final shape of suburban street grids was thus the result of a cumulation of builders' decisions which balanced their desires for the least street area with their desires for the most frontage lots

Some sort of evaluation of what kind of houses were to go on the land determined the subdividers' choice between the two alternatives. Houses for the central segment of the middle class required a fairly ample lot so that there would be room for the generous floor area of the house, some separation from its neighbors, and lawn and garden space to the front and rear. Developers intending to attract customers for such houses needed all the land area they could get. Lower middle class housing, on the other hand, took less first floor area, and, in order to keep costs down, less land. In this case many narrow frontage lots were the best answer to the customer's habits and the developer's profit.

One of the enduring attractions of the frontage lot and grid system lies in its flexibility: a layout conceived for one kind of purchaser can often be reworked to meet the needs of a different one. As lower-income groups moved out over suburban land subdividers holding unsold parcels could adjust their lots to meet these new customers. No rearrangement of streets was required. For example, a man who divided several blocks into lots 50 by 90 feet for medium-priced singles and doubles could reslice these same lots for different users. By reducing the total area per lot he could keep down the customer's land costs and sometimes help himself to a higher mark-up. In the example given if the lots were narrowed to a width of 35 or 40 feet, the standard cheap single and two-family house lot emerged. A further narrowing to 27 or 30 feet produced the standard three-decker lot. In a period of rapid urban growth and rapid change in the income characteristics of neighborhoods, this flexible quality of the grid street and frontage lot system of land division was of great use to land traders.

In the suburbs the laying out of streets and the division and re-division of the blocks into various sizes went on without much governmental supervision. As speculators went about their business the grids were laid out on a parcel-by-parcel basis and each filed with the county Registry of Deeds. Since there was no overall layout of the streets, as in the Back Bay, there was not a single grid in the suburbs, but rather an aggregation of grid farms. The manner in which the grid farm was connected to its neighbor depended upon the historical conditions that faced the developer at the time of the original subdivision.

From 1870 to 1891 the Board of Street Commissioners was the official body charged with the supervision of street layout in Boston. Because the board lacked the power to establish street lines prior to any municipal seizure of private land, its actions were entirely negative. The principal role of the Street Commissioners was to decide whether or not to accept private streets for public maintenance. For many years Boston mayors complained of the want of efficient supervision, especially the bad results this easy-going policy had upon traffic movement and drainage problems. In the downtown area, where traffic loads grew heavier every year and filled land gave drainage difficulties, the city was put to considerable expense to widen and re-grade streets whose initial layout proved unsatisfactory to later users.[19]

By and large the suburbs were never the primary source of street problems, because here the widespread use of the forty-foot street provided ample surface for traffic, and most of the building took place on easily drained high ground.[20] Under these circumstances the creation in 1891 of a specific supervisory agency, the Board of Survey, brought no notable change in suburban subdivision and street layout. The informal, privately planned grid street and frontage lot remained the constant and universal system of land division throughout the years 1870–1900.

Suburban Architecture

The web of forces that sustained the grid street and frontage lot land division—the inherited popular standards, the municipal policy, the requirements of speculators—could not have brought about the universal use of grids had there not been a harmony between this method of land division and the popular architecture of the day. Thus, from about 1820 to 1873 the formal row house and grid street predominated. In the central city almost all residential construction, with the exception of the cheapest tenements and an occasional mansion, followed this architectural idea. In the peripheral towns the same fashion was frequently copied, both in brick and wood. Subdividers laid out patches of regular grids and clumps of row houses next to tiny citified parks even though acres of land lay vacant about their projects.[21]

Nevertheless, even during the years 1820 to 1873 a minority practice continued earlier housing customs. Especially in the peripheral towns, and on the hills and valleys beyond these villages, there had existed since the eighteenth century alternatives to the city row house: the local merchant's and artisan's wooden detached single house, and the estate of the wealthy Bostonian.

In the late eighteenth and early nineteenth centuries, no substantial break in architecture divided city from country houses. Georgian models dominated both, and it was personal taste that decided whether the rich man's country seat or his town house was more elaborate. Harrison Gray Otis chose the city for his greatest expenditures; the Gores, on the other hand, constructed a lavish country hall. The little wooden houses that lined the villages were farm houses adorned with current city fashions in ornament, and like their city equivalents they changed from Georgian to classic revival, to more romantic details as style dictated.

In some measure this all-pervasive spread of ornament continued throughout the century, but with the growth of the central city there developed, despite any continuity of detail, a sharp break between the basic architecture of the city and its periphery. In the city close living increased. The building of street after street of row houses created in the Boston of the 1850's an area of a mile or two in diameter which

FIG. 57. Classic Revival house of the second quarter of the nineteenth century. Inexpensive single-family house of lower Roxbury's peripheral town era

was clearly a city landscape. Mid-century Boston was a solid expanse of shops, factories, and houses which every year grew larger. Beginning with the first appearance of this large urban space, and perhaps partly in reaction to it, the romantic movement captured the minds of architects and builders. In Greater Boston this romanticism usually took the architectural form of further elaboration of classical ornament, and from the 1850's to the 1870's a widespread use of heavy Italianate detail. Perhaps the strong local classical tradition, so well stated by the Boston architect Bulfinch, prevented gothic styles from ever becoming the dominant manifestation of romantic architecture.

The whole purpose and feeling of the new architecture, however, was different from the previous styles. In 1820 the peripheral towns were to some extent lesser versions of the city. By 1850 the entire architectural environment had changed. No amount of romantic ornament could make a cottage out of a city row house. At the same time, upper middle class commuters had firmly established an alternative to city living. Instead of a Georgian mansion complete with all the appurtenances of a town house, the new estates of the wealthy were romantic retreats furnished and landscaped in terms of the new statement of the rural ideal.[22] Not only did the shift in architectural style and the growth of the city increase the contrast between city and country, but every year brought more widespread participation in nonurban living. The railroad, the omnibus, and the horsecar accompanied the change in style. With these new devices many wealthy estate owners took to living in the peripheral towns all year round, and numerous upper middle class families moved out into suburban areas.

Sometime during the 1860's or 1870's the balance of forces shifted. During the last third of the nineteenth century the suburban styles became the majority practice and the town row house became the minority one. Except for continued construction in the Back Bay the row house became a thing of the past. The attraction of the rural ideal and the continued press of industrialization and immigration turned the middle class against city living as it had been known in the past.

The architecture of the 1870–1900 period partook of two forces: a

Fig. 58. Typical railroad commuter's Romantic-Classical house, c. 1850

negative force, the discrediting of previous urban styles; and a positive force, the creation of a specifically suburban style which was both adapted to previous middle class city traditions and suited to some of the goals of the rural ideal.

The social history of old central Boston neighborhoods gave a strong negative drive to middle class acceptance of new housing styles. The last active manifestation of row housing with uniform façade was the mansard, or Second Empire style, of the 1860's and 1870's. As a style it lost favor after 1873 from being identified with the speculative excesses of the postwar boom. During the next twelve years, while construction proceeded at a much reduced pace, the fashionable center of Boston shifted from Beacon Hill and the South End to the Back Bay. This move to the Back Bay by the upper middle class was not just a search for a new façade for row houses; rather it was a mass exodus before the advance of industry, commerce, and immigrants. By 1885 the South End had become a lower class and lodging-house section, and Beacon Hill was badly weakened in its social tone. With conversions of row housing going on all over the city during the 1880's and 1890's the row house became for the middle class a symbol of financial failure and bad neighborhoods.

The contemporary course of building in the three towns of Roxbury, West Roxbury, and Dorchester demonstrates the positive force exerted by the development of a new suburban architecture. The period from 1860 to 1875 was one of architectural confusion. Scattered imitations of town row housing were built for commuters moving out to Roxbury. The inner sections of the three towns also received little wooden detached houses finished in the popular mansard style for modernists, or in older and simpler classical ornament for the conservatives. In the more distant parts of Dorchester and West Roxbury expensive gothic, Italianate, and mansard houses were built on large quarter- and half-acre lots. Here too, developers tried occasional medium-priced imitations, little cottages placed on generous lots of 5,000 square feet.

The sudden exodus of large numbers of middle class families used to city living caused these unsettled architectural conditions. In the 1840's and 1850's when relatively small numbers of middle class families had moved to the suburbs they had done so out of a clear preference for a rural setting. Their gothic cottages and Italianate houses, all set on ample garden plots, witness their intention. Now, when the central segment of the middle class was moving from the city, less land was available to each family. At the same time the lower income of the newcomers reduced potential lot sizes.

Also, the new commuter's choice of the rural ideal was a less clear one. He probably wished to imitate his predecessors, but he was also a refugee from city conditions. Though favorable to some sort of country life he wanted to continue to enjoy city services and he desired an architecture which would provide some of the effect of the row house façade—the public presentation of an impression of wealth and social standing.

The shingle style architects answered this desire for some kind of building which would contain both the tone of the rural ideal and the symbolic formality of town housing. The timing of the new school's transformation of domestic architecture was a happy one; the peak of its activity took place during the years 1870–1885. In these years Henry H. Richardson, one of the most fashionable and skillful practitioners of the new style, built many houses in metropolitan Boston. His work attracted numerous followers. The previous gothic and Italianate houses in the suburbs had strong rural referents and high requirements of land. The new shingle style, on the other hand, embodied a very flexible concept of a house, a house whose main tone was individual, prosperous, private, and suburban.[23]

A short walk down one of the fashionable streets of the period will demonstrate the architectural progress of the suburb. On Townsend street in Roxbury there stands a block of houses which illustrates the changes in postwar upper middle class styles. At number 174 there is a good example of the transitional years of the 1860's and early 1870's: a square romantic-classical house onto which has been grafted the popular mansard roof. Just up the street, at number 140–142, is the new suburban shingle style house. This house dates from the 1890's but its shingle and stone work mark it as a continuation of the best sort of suburban house of the late 1870's and 1880's. Looking at this house one can see that it needs no rural setting or special landscaping to be effective. It needs room, for it spreads out, but as a big house on a small lot it achieves all the grandeur of the older styles, while at the same time provides a completely flexible interior space that could be fitted to the requirements of the individual owner's domestic life. Number 140–142 is unusual for being an elegant double house, vertically divided and designed to look like a single. The room arrangements and use of bays and conservatories are different for each unit.

Flexibility of design was a characteristic of the suburban shingle style. The individual planning of interior spaces to fit the client's domestic life was a manifestation of the strong contemporary interest in private family life. The equivalent Back Bay structures had extensive ornamental variation, but the narrow lots of row housing prevented any but two or three interior plans. By contrast, a move to the suburbs in the 1880's offered the upper middle class family the pleasant prospect of an individually designed interior as well as a unique exterior.

Numbers 123 and 144 on Townsend street are examples of the abandonment of the inventive shingle style and the return in the

Fig. 59. The transitional suburban house. Square Romantic-Classical house with mansard roof, c. 1860. Number 174 Townsend street

Fig. 60. Suburban shingle style house c. 1890. Number 140–142 Townsend street, an unusual custom designed duplex

Fig. 61. Colonial Revival, c. 1895: number 144 Townsend street

Fig. 62. Colonial Revival, c. 1895: number 123 Townsend street

1890's to classical forms. It is important to note, however, that these houses do not represent the later twentieth century extreme in which careful reconstruction of old buildings was sought after. These dwellings of the 1890's offer no special limitations to the desires of the owner. Also, as far as the public was concerned, these houses, like the shingle style ones, were suburban houses; that is, houses designed with their most important side toward the street. The effect of the design did not, however, depend on any specially landscaped lot. With their concentration on the façade and flexible interior all these upper middle class houses provided fashion models ready for copying in a range of scales and prices to suit all suburban pocketbooks.

Expensive houses of the late nineteenth century were eminently suited to many of the requirements of all levels of middle class building; they emphasized the street façade in a way which made the new architecture suitable to small frontage lots, and they all implied prosperity. The work of suburban builders during the 1870–1900 period was full of borrowings from expensive models. The medium-priced single or two-family house changed from a clapboard house with romantic-classical detail, to a shingled house with turrets, eves, and gables, and then back to classical ornament again. Even the three-decker, which began its career in the 1880's laden with fancy shingle work in imitation of the millionaire's "cottage," was by 1900 fitted out with classical columns and pilasters.

More important than the handing down of fashionable ornament from one income group to the next was the extensive imitation of the style of life the ornament implied. Beginning perhaps with the transitional Second Empire houses, and certainly with the shingle-style houses, there was a shift in emphasis from the prior romantic rural forms. These postwar houses were at once more public and more imposing than their predecessors, and, at the same time they bespoke a continuing emphasis on a private family life. These houses of the last third of the nineteenth century are clearly suburbanized, they no longer depend upon rural nature or an estate-sized lot for their effect. Indeed, they achieve their imposing quality by being large houses arranged in big masses on relatively small lots. In an era so devoted

FIG. 63. Medium-priced, shingle style, one-family house, 1884

FIG. 64. Single-door, shingle style, two-family house, 1881

FIG. 65. Shingle style, one-family house with oriental doorway, c. 1895

to private money-making it seems hardly an accident that streets of row houses with more or less identical swell fronts were abandoned for a suburban style of individualized houses, arranged in such a way as to produce for the public the gratifying view of a prosperous street.

The speed and unanimity with which the new architecture was taken up by the mass of builders serves as a further demonstration of the discipline of the individual agents of city building. The ultimate cause of uniform behavior among suburban builders lay in the relationship between these small agents and the environment in which they worked—the relationship between small amateur investors and the immediate forces of architectural fashions, the grid street and frontage lot tradition, and the real estate market. Because the agents of the suburban building process operated on such a limited scale the popular conceptions of the new suburban architecture and the grid

FIG. 66. An early Colonial Revival three-decker, 1897

street and frontage lot system dominated builders' decisions and set limits upon their choices.

As small investors, men with severely limited sums at their disposal, each decision of when, where, and what to build had to make an immediate profit for the decision maker or he would soon go bankrupt. No widely traded commodity of the period was bought and sold in such expensive minimum units as the $2,000 to $10,000 house and lot. The many homeowners building for the first time, either for their own use or for the use of others, tended to be anxious followers of regular procedures because of this large capital requirement. Professional speculators also lacked freedom of choice. It required most of their skill and energy to guess the right year, the right lot, and the right house, and then to push the project through the hazards of financing, building, and sale. Because of this heavy personal financial commitment within a field of considerable risk professionals and amateurs uniformly clung to traditional and popular methods in order to make their profits more certain.

CHAPTER SEVEN

THE CONSEQUENCES

TWO QUALITIES mark off the Boston of 1900 from all preceding eras: its great size and its new suburban arrangement. In 1850 the metropolitan region of Boston encompassed a radius of but two or three miles, a population of two hundred thousand; in 1900 the region extended over a ten-mile radius and contained a population of more than a million. A change in structure accompanied this change in scale. Once a dense merchant city clustered about an ocean port, Boston became a sprawling industrial metropolis. In 1850 it was a fairly small and unified area, by 1900 it had split into two functional parts: an industrial, commercial, and communications center packed tight against the port, and an enormous outer suburban ring of residences and industrial and commercial subcenters. By examining in detail the method of building one part of the great outer suburban ring, this book has attempted to discover something about the society that underwent this transformation, and to elicit some of the consequences of this new physical arrangement of people.

In Roxbury, West Roxbury, and Dorchester the parade of 23,000 new houses arranged by grid streets and frontage lots, the regular progress from one architectural style to the next, the constancy of basic house design, and the clustering of buildings by the income levels of their owners witness uniformity of behavior among individual decision makers.

Both positive and negative factors contributed to the uniformity of decisions of the 9,000 private builders. Positively, these middle class homeowners and amateur investors shared a sympathy for the suburban style of living which was then developing in metropolitan Boston. There existed a consensus of attitude which made each decision maker to some degree favorable to the new shingle and later colonial revival styles of architecture. This same consensus caused each man to build houses much like those of his neighbors and to seek to locate in a neighborhood or on a street which was popular with families of an income similar to his own. Finally, this same consensus encouraged each man to seek and to perpetuate the new suburban environment which emphasized the pleasures of private family life, the security of a small community setting, and the enjoyments of an increased contact with nature. The strength of this consensus grew with the passage of time. Every year more and more middle class families lived in the suburbs. Every year, too, the streetcar and utility networks brought a steady increase in land available for settlement so that successively closer approximations to the desired environment became possible.

Negatively, suburban builders were repelled by conditions in the central city. The unending immigrant invasion, the conversion of old houses and the encroachment of industry and commerce heightened the contrast between the new suburbs and the central city. Negatively, too, the limited financial position of homebuilders disciplined their choices of houses and neighborhoods and controlled their methods of land division.

The policies of the large institutions concerned with building supported and disciplined these individual choices. The role of the larger agents was essential. At the municipal scale, utilities had to be laid before most men would be willing to build. Adequate streetcar service also preceded homebuilders and their customers. At the neighborhood scale the arrival of new families attracted by a new improved transportation service, or the expansion of adjacent neighborhoods, or the departure of old families because of housing obsolescence, all encouraged one kind of building and discouraged others. At his peril a man built cheap rental units in outer suburbs, or expensive singles in old inner suburbs. The patterned spread of various kinds of new construction bears witness to the power of the informal neighborhood regulation of building. It was a power based upon the sensitivity of individual landowners to the economic standing of their neighbors.

The behavior of the large institutions concerned with suburban building also encouraged individual landowners to repeat in their building the popular suburban architecture, engineering, and economic grading of neighborhoods. Late nineteenth century Boston was a fast-growing metropolitan society made prosperous by the new industrial technology and propelled by the energy of thousands of individual capitalists. The middle class was one of the principal beneficiaries of this prosperity, and its well-being and rapid enlargement gave this large segment of Boston society the confidence to stress its equalitarianism and the willingness to exploit each new technological device. The rise of thousands of families of the most diverse ethnic backgrounds to a middle class competence, like their quick adoption of each new invention, was taken as proof of the success of the society.

The City of Boston and the later metropolitan boards enthusiastically adopted the new sanitary engineering. These institutions undertook to see that all new neighborhoods would be built to the latest standards, and at great expense attempted to service the old parts of the city. This enormous undertaking not only made the new devices available to Boston's homeowners, but also stimulated the universal acceptance of middle class criteria for home services. In the suburbs all the new regulations for plumbing, gas fitting, and building and fire safety were perhaps more important as official affirmations of middle class norms than for policing an occasional offender. With the cooperation and example of the large institutions almost all new suburban building from 1870 to 1900 included safe construction, indoor plumbing, and orderly land arrangement. From the prosperity of the middle class and its enthusiastic acceptance of the new sanitation and transportation technology came the popular achievement of the late nineteenth century suburbs: a safe environment for half the metropolitan population.

The orientation of the large institutions toward the benefit of the suburban builders also assisted the small landowners. The street railways and other utilities rapidly extended their service to outlying metropolitan villages. In so doing they encouraged private development of distant land. This policy was aimed at taking advantage of the general growth of the city, but it also reflected a belief that public agencies should assist private undertakings. Similarly, the Park Department carefully avoided land which was thought to be suited to private construction, taking instead the marshes and uplands at the edge of areas then building. In effect, the Park Department landscaped the margins of private developments. In the new neighborhoods the City of Boston built schools at a very rapid rate and its official architecture and landscape design mirrored the fashions of private builders. Public policy held installation charges for new utilities and streets to below cost, much of the expense being borne by general taxation and general rates. When the city bargained with gas and electric companies for the extension of its lighting it often bargained in behalf of residential users as well, endeavoring to see that they too would be connected to the new lines and served at reasonable rates.[1] The combined effect of all these policies was to greatly assist the individual builder to develop the vacant land outside the old city.

At the level of homeowners' decisions the class character of neighborhoods played a more supportive than immediately disciplinary role. Though the migration of various income groups ultimately determined the uses, rents, and fate of neighborhoods, at the moment of construction the power of regulation lay only in the example set by the behavior of others. The presence of houses of similar cost and style encouraged a man to build his own house in keeping with existing ones. No laws, however, prevented him from building something different.

The variety of ethnic backgrounds of families living within the surrounding houses also encouraged the builder of a new house to minimize any ethnic hostilities he might possess. If no Catholic, Methodist, or Episcopal church yet existed in his neighborhood the presence of recently built churches and schools all over the suburbs allowed a new resident to expect one soon. Just as curbs and gas lights might still be a few years in coming to his street, so, too, the arrival of his particular church, club, and school, was merely a matter of time.

To all these characteristics—the speed of building, the mass arrival of new families, the separation of families by economic class, the universality of the new high standards of light, air, land, and sanitation —must be added the effect of the omnipresent newness. Whether a man lived in a lower middle class quarter of cheap three-deckers, or on a fashionable street of expensive singles, the latest styles, the freshly painted houses, the neat streets, the well-kept lawns, and the new schools and parks gave him a sense of confidence in the success of his society and a satisfaction at his participation in it. These physical expressions gave him the willingness to abide by the rules of the society whether the rules took the form of building regulations or the less specific directions of group imitation. The very extent of newness in the suburbs, which by 1900 dwarfed the old central city, made these areas a source of pride for Boston's metropolitan society. Today suburbs are increasingly assigned all the evils of American society; but in the late nineteenth century they created a widespread sense of achievement.

The general contemporary satisfaction with suburbs came from their ability to answer some of the major needs of the day. To be sure, the costs of new construction were such as to exclude at least half the families of Boston; but the suburban half, the middle class, was the dominant class in the society. To middle class families the suburbs gave a safe, sanitary environment, new houses in styles somewhat in keeping with their conception of family life, and temporary neighborhoods of people with similar outlook. In an atmosphere of rapid change, the income-graded neighborhoods rendered two important services to their residents. Evenness of wealth meant neighbors who would reinforce an individual family's efforts to pass on its values to its children. The surrounding evenness of wealth also gave adults a sense of a community of shared experience, and thereby gave some measure of relief from the uncertainties inherent in a world of highly competitive capitalism.

In addition to benefiting their own residents, in one important way the suburbs served the half of Boston's population which could not afford them. The apparent openness of the new residential quarters, their ethnic variety, their extensive growth, and their wide range of prices from fairly inexpensive rental suites to expensive single-family houses—these visible characteristics of the new suburbs gave aspiring low-income families the certainty that should they earn enough money they too could possess the comforts and symbols of success. Even for those excluded from them, the suburbs offered a physical demonstration that the rewards of competitive capitalism might be within the reach of all.

The rendering of these important social services gave Bostonians of the late nineteenth century a confidence that at least in the suburbs they had struck a successful compromise among the conflicts then active in their society. The suburban city, however, was a compromise which had all the faults of its virtues. Many of the same devices that gave power and dynamism to its building contained within them unresolved conflicts. These conflicts, in turn, worked to destroy much of what the suburb hoped to achieve.

Homeownership was one suburban goal, but the high down payments and short-term, nonamortizing mortgages of the unregulated mortgage market restricted homeownership to one quarter of Boston's families. A pleasant landscape was another goal, but the lack of training and limited financial capabilities of subdividers condemned the new streetcar suburbs to the progressive destruction of their natural setting. Under the grid street and frontage lot system of land division natural contours were thrown away for the short-term advantages of easy marketing and cheap utility and street construction. Once all the narrow lots had been occupied, a band of tiny front lawns and a row of street trees was about all the verdure a suburban development could offer.

The suburb, the home of property owners and settled family life, was thought by contemporaries to be an environment that encouraged individual participation in community life. Compared to transient conditions in older parts of the city the suburbs were more conducive to integration of the individual into some sort of community activity.[2] Their physical arrangement, however—the endless street grids and the dependence upon the downtown for work and shopping—failed to provide local centers where all the residents of a given area might, through frequent contact, come to know each other and thereby be encouraged to share in community-wide activities.

Aside from class segregation there was nothing in the process of late nineteenth century suburban construction that built communities or neighborhoods: it built streets. The grid plan of the suburbs did not concern itself with public life. It was an economically efficient geometry which divided large parcels of land as they came on the market. The arrangement of the blocks of the grid depended largely upon what farm or estate came on the market at what time. The result was not integrated communities arranged about common centers, but a historical and accidental traffic pattern.

Where a railroad station and arterial streets came together, stores, churches, and sometimes schools were built to serve some of the needs of the residents of the area. In Dorchester, for example, there were historic village clusters that grew with the increase of population around them: Meeting House Hill, Harrison Square, Codman Square, Lower Mills. Other clusters—such as Fields Corner, Grove Hall, and Columbia Square—were largely the work of the new streetcar transportation network. Most characteristic of the new suburban order was the commercial strip which followed the main transportation lines and had no center at all. Washington street, Dorchester, from Codman Square to Grove Hall lacked any historic center. It was simply a long row of little stores which served those passing by and those living in the houses behind.

This centerless tendency was intensified by the Boston School Department's building policy which placed schools on inexpensive land on the side streets. In this way the schools formed partial centers by themselves which were often isolated from the commercial and social centers. The most dramatic example was the placing of Dorchester High School in Ashmont with the consequent destruction of the town's old educational center at Meeting House Hill. Roxbury High School was similarly mislocated. In West Roxbury, however, the school building policy maintained the historic center at Eliot Square. By this municipal money-saving policy the child of the suburbs was isolated from the center of his community in the same way his mother was separated from her husband's work.

An amorphous and weak neighborhood structure was the consequence of compounding communities with a mix of side-street grids, commercial strips, and small historic centers. A family living near the corner of Tonawanda street and Geneva avenue in central Dorchester during the 1890's shopped locally on Geneva avenue, and went to Boston for major purchases. If they happened to be Congregationalists their church stood on their corner. The father went to Boston on the Old Colony Railroad or took the streetcar down Dorchester avenue. The children went to primary school, however, in a different neighborhood on the other side of Dorchester avenue. If the family was not Congregational they had to go to a third neighborhood for church, and, of course, social clubs were scattered through the town. A similar family living twelve doors up Tonawanda street had an entirely different orientation. Its business area lay along the Washington street strip.

As a result of the centerless character of most suburbs, community life fell into fragments. Groups formed about particular churches, clubs, schools, and ward club rooms; rarely did any large fraction of the population of a suburban area participate in any joint endeavor. When, through accident, the historic political boundaries of a town coincided with the building pattern of a new suburb local politics provided a framework for community activities. Nevertheless, even these conditions were unfavorable to the development of meaningful community life. The limited subject matter of town politics, and the frequently narrow income band of the residents of new bedroom suburbs, together generated an enervating parochialism which hung heavy over such community life as existed.[3]

In 1900 the new metropolis lacked local communities that could deal with the problems of contemporary society at the level of the family and its immediate surroundings, and it lacked a large-scale community that could deal with the problems of the metropolis.[4] As a result Boston community life fell into a self-defeating cycle. Each decade brought an increase in the scale and complexity of economic and social life; each decade's problems demanded more wide-scale attention, more complex solutions. Because of the physical arrangement of the new metropolis, each decade also brought an ever greater fragmentation of community life into town and ward politics, church groups, clubs, and specialized societies of all kinds. The growing parochialism and fragmentation resulted in a steady relative weakening of social agencies. Weakness, in turn, convinced more and more individuals that local community action was hopeless or irrelevant. From this conviction came the further weakening of the public agencies. The self-defeating cycle, begun by the streetcar metropolis, has continued with increasing severity to this day. It has proved, both for the metropolis and its constituent political units, an iron cycle, a cycle which once established, is difficult to break.

The inattention of late nineteenth century Bostonians to the fragmentation of their community life was not an accidental oversight, it was a matter of principle, the principle of individualistic capitalism. Above all else the streetcar suburbs stand as a monument to a society which wished to keep the rewards of capitalist competition open to all its citizens. Despite ignorance and prejudice, during this period of mass immigration, the suburbs remained open to all who could meet the price.

By 1900 about half the families of metropolitan Boston had come to share this new environment. The wealth brought to the society by its industrial technology, and the special practices of suburban building, made this mass achievement possible. The manner in which the nineteenth century building process physically separated the metropolitan population into two sections—the middle class section of families who could afford new construction, and the lower class section of families who could not—assisted some of the open equalitarian goals of the capitalist society. In the suburbs families of similar economic standing lived next to each other, and their similarity of economic position helped them to learn to ignore their differences of religion and national background. The great extent of the new suburbs, moreover, left room for fine gradations of the middle class population. Middle class families were free to choose among hundreds of possible locations, free to find a neighborhood which suited both their ethnic feelings and their progress up the economic ladder.

The infrangible and enduring problems of the suburbs also derive from the principle of open capitalist competition. At any moment in the late nineteenth century half the metropolitan society was not successful, half the society remained apart from the achievements of the suburbs. The process of new construction, since it was tied to the abilities of individual builders erecting houses for their own immediate use or profit, took no effective responsibility for the lower income half of the society. As a result, contemporary progress in housing for lower class families was slow and uncertain, limited to slight improvements in sanitation, structural safety, and fire prevention.

By sheer enlargement of their numbers, and by the obsolescence of middle-income structures, low-income groups could and did reach the new suburbs. Most often, however, they could occupy them only by destroying much of what the suburb had achieved. Because the late-comers possessed but small sums for rent, secondhand houses in the suburbs often had to be divided and redivided so that a single became a double or a triple, to a two-family house was added an attic apartment, and so forth. Even where slightly higher incomes made division of structures unnecessary the cost of maintaining old wooden houses often prevented the newcomers from keeping up their houses and lots to the level originally intended. Though not included in their rent bills, the progressive deterioration of their environment was one of the prices of low-income tenancy.[5]

Neither the architecture nor the land planning of the new suburbs took any account of the possible subsequent users. A satisfactory single-family house brought, when divided, two or three cramped and mean apartments, each one often well below the building's original standards for light, air, and sanitation. The reduction in floor area per person brought an immediate and obvious retreat from the norms of the first owner. The garden setting of the street often disappeared under the feet of running children; back yards and porches filled with the overflow and trash from the houses; planted playgrounds required tar to support increased use; and the large country parks grew to weeds because of lack of time and interest among their new users.

By assigning building to the activities of thousands of individual middle class landowners the metropolitan society allowed itself to build a physical environment which would become, by its own terms, the unsatisfactory home of half its members. By this means also the society received a physical plan which was destructive to its democratic processes. The essence of the new metropolitan plan was the separation of the vast areas of new construction from the old central city.

The literature of late nineteenth century reformers tells the consequences of this division. For the middle class the inner area of low-income housing became an unknown and uncontrolled land. Here, in one ward vice and drunkenness flourished out of reach of middle class supervision; in another ward nationalist demagogues, institutionally isolated from the rest of the metropolis and responsible only to the majority of the ward, held free rein in the search for their own profit. Such troublesome manifestations of the divided society gave much concern to contemporaries. They were but symptoms of the serious consequences of the physical division of classes.

Most important, the concentration in a solid two-mile area of foreign languages, poverty, sweatshops, and slum housing gave the suburban middle class a sense of hopelessness and fear. Much of the work of reformers in the twentieth century progressive era had to be devoted to the task of educating the middle class to the conditions of modern industrial cities. It was a task undertaken with the middle class faith that through knowledge would come a willingness to take action.[6]

Opposing reformers' goals of knowledge and action stood the structure of the streetcar metropolis which had damaged the fabric of the society. In part the rural ideal bore responsibility for the arrangement of the metropolis, for it had encouraged middle class families to seek escape from the conditions of modern industrial life into an isolated family environment. More important, the dominant ideal of individualistic capitalism with its accompanying unwillingness to bring private profit to account had caused the economic division of the society. The slums and the suburbs were the physical expression of this division. The conditions of the central city which so dismayed the middle class were the product of its failure to control the distribution of income, its failure to regulate housing and working conditions, its failure to develop an adequate welfare program for the sick and unfortunate, and its failure to devise a community program for integrating the thousands of new citizens who every year moved to the metropolis. These things, neglected, bore a harvest of middle class fear. From fear came the late nineteenth century paradox of the growth of an economically integrated regional city of over a million inhabitants accompanied by an increase in the parochialism of its political and social units.

In 1870 many middle class suburbanites regarded Boston as their achievement, something they wished to join in order to create a political union of homes, jobs, and community. Such sentiment gave popularity to the mid-century annexation movement. From about 1850 to 1873 almost every city and town around Boston had an annexationist group, and the question of the advantages and disadvantages of union with Boston was seriously debated. In 1868 Roxbury joined Boston; in 1870 Dorchester, and in 1873 Charlestown, Brighton, and West Roxbury, voted for unification.

The year 1873 marked the end of the annexation movement. That year the residents of Brookline voted to remain separate. This political defeat, and the Depression of 1873–1878 ended public concern over the metropolitan expansion of Boston. With the return of prosperity, however, the movement never revived. Instead, the legislature created in the late 1880's and early 1890's three specialized state-managed agencies which undertook to serve metropolitan needs for water, sewer, and park building.

The sudden and permanent collapse of the annexation movement had two causes: the first concerned municipal services; the second, the idea of community. During the middle years of the nineteenth century some of the larger and more prosperous of the peripheral towns and cities had built their own waterworks and expanded their street and educational services so that they approximated some of the high standards of Boston. In 1870 Charlestown, Cambridge, and Brookline had satisfactory independent waterworks. These same towns and Dorchester and Roxbury possessed advanced educational facilities. Other towns, however, lacked the tax base and access to the rivers and lakes necessary for high-quality municipal service. The metropolitan agencies, by building a unified drainage and water supply for the whole metropolis, put all the region's towns in a position to meet modern municipal standards.

The motive of services having been withdrawn, there remained only the idea of community. Annexation debates had always concerned themselves with this question. Annexationists appealed to the idea of one great city where work and home, social and cultural activities, industry, and commerce would be joined in a single political union. Boston, they said, would share the fate of Rome if the middle class, which heretofore had provided the governance of the city and the force of its reforms, abandoned the city for the suburbs.[7]

Opponents of annexation countered with the ideal of small town life: the simple informal community, the town meeting, the maintenance of the traditions of rural New England. They held out to their audience the idea of the suburban town as a refuge from the pressures of the new industrial metropolis. Nor were the opponents of annexation slow to point out that the high level of city services maintained by Boston meant higher taxes, and further, they frankly stated that independent suburban towns could maintain native American life free from Boston's waves of incoming poor immigrants.[8]

As early as 1851 West Roxbury estate owners led a successful move to separate the rural part of the town of Roxbury from its industrial half. In 1873 middle class Boston commuters who had moved to West Roxbury reversed this decision by a close vote, and the town joined Boston. The new commuters wanted the high level of services offered by Boston, and they were confident that the middle class could govern the enlarged city to its own satisfaction.

By the 1880's, with but one exception, no suburban town ever again seriously considered annexation.[9] The segregation of the metropolitan population brought about by the interaction of the expansion of street railway transportation and the suburban building process had by the mid-1880's given a permanent set to political life. In the face of the continually expanding size of the metropolis, by contrast to the continual waves of poor immigrants that flooded the central city and destroyed its old residential neighborhoods, the new suburbs offered ever new areas of homogeneous middle class settlement. Here, most immigrants spoke English, most were Americanized, and here the evenness of income lessened the scope of political conflict. It was already apparent in the 1880's that to join Boston was to assume all the burdens and conflicts of a modern industrial metropolis. To remain apart was to escape, at least for a time, some of these problems. In the face of this choice the metropolitan middle class abandoned their central city.

Very soon the middle class began to reap the harvest of its action. Already by 1900 Boston was something to be feared and controlled. Many of its powers of self-government had been taken from it by the state or voluntarily abandoned by tax-conscious voters to put a check on demands for public improvements.[10] Beyond Boston the special suburban form of popularly managed local government continued to flourish. In suburbs of substantial income and limited class structure, high standards of education and public service were often achieved. Each town, however, now managed its affairs as best it could surrounded by forces largely beyond its control. New transportation, new housing, new industries, new people, the great flow and vigor of the metropolis, lay beyond the knowledge and competence of these individual agencies. In the years to come World Wars and depressions would unleash antidemocratic forces that threatened the foundations of the society: its democratic institutions, its property, its ethnic harmony, the chance of each citizen to prosper through capitalist competition. Confronting these challenges stood a metropolitan society physically divided by classes, politically divided by about forty parochial institutions. So divided, the society denied itself the opportunity to end, through common action against common problems, the isolation of its citizens and the fear they held toward each other. So divided, the metropolis was helpless to solve its own problems.

During the years 1870 to 1900 industrial capitalism was, comparatively, a new thing, and a mass suburban metropolis like Boston had never existed before anywhere in the world. To rely on individual capitalists, to expect that each man building for himself would build a good environment for a democratic society was perhaps a reasonable error to have made. Today, some of the problems confronting the streetcar city have been solved or passed by. Except for the American Negro, immigration conditions are over. The automobile allows a less rigid class arrangement and less dense housing than was possible under streetcar transportation. Zoning, large-scale subdivision planning, and new financial institutions have made suburban building somewhat more orderly, and have opened homeownership to a greater proportion of the society. Most important of all, the great twentieth century national reforms of progressive taxation and labor, factory, and welfare legislation have allowed more widespread participation in the profits of industrialism.

Despite these changes the two great problems first met in the streetcar city remain unsolved. Even by popular standards one enormous segment of the population still lives in an unsatisfactory physical environment. More serious, because it is a condition which affects all others, the growing metropolitan society as a whole remains shut up in an ever larger number of specialized social and political units, its citizens isolated from one another, its society needlessly uncontrolled because of the weakness of its agents.

APPENDIXES

BIBLIOGRAPHICAL NOTE

NOTES · INDEX

APPENDIX A

A LOCAL HISTORIAN'S GUIDE TO SOCIAL STATISTICS

The world is full of Roxburys and Dorchesters; places statesmen never visited, towns and counties upon whose single fate no intellectual movement or nation has as yet depended. The Roxburys and Dorchesters of the world outnumber both the Florences and the Lexingtons. The sheer numbers of these commonplace and anonymous districts should excite historians' curiosity, but their claim for study transcends the mere fact of neglect.

In these times the world often seems beset by large and anonymous forces, forces both unintelligible and ungovernable. The identification and understanding of such forces constitutes one of the principal tasks of modern scholars. Many concepts have been and are being tried: class, mobility, mechanization, urbanization, and the like. In order to clarify such concepts and develop new ones scholars must establish the link between the concepts themselves and the experiences of the men and women who lived in the past. The small area of concern of local history makes it an exceedingly promising field for the development of just this sort of historical material.

A modern social scientist can construct a questionnaire and interview his subjects; he cannot, however, place his concept in time without the aid of historical data. The social scientist needs the answers to many questions. Is urbanization as we now think of it new or old? Is mechanization by computer-programmed machines more or less destructive to established work habits and institutions than mechanization by water power? In large measure the accuracy of the interpretation of most of our current concepts of social behavior depends upon the delineation of the differences and similarities of the past.

In addition to his role as a social scientist the local historian has an important public function which, at present, he rarely performs. There is currently a desperate need for the establishment of meaningful local traditions. The need is world-wide. The giant metropolitan suburb, like Brooklyn, New York, the ancient town, like York, England, or the Southern city undergoing the latest kind of industrialization, like Spartanburg, South Carolina, all lack a meaningful tradition which could place in focus the environment now experienced by local residents. Myths that confuse and distort present reality exist for all such places. Generally they are myths written by representatives of some ethnic group or class which by pleasant half-truths recall some Golden Age—the "good old days" in Brooklyn before the Jews, or Negroes, or Puerto Ricans; the glory that was York-minster; the stirring times of the Civil War. The millions of people who live in such places and who must cope with the complexities and confusions of modern life deserve better of their historians. They deserve accurate narratives of the entire range of past experience of their cities and towns; narratives whose focus is an explanation of the present and whose method is the elucidation of concrete detail from the past. The writing of such narratives is the important function of the local historian.

To write such local histories the historian must learn more about a town, or county, or city, than the actions of its politicians and leading families. He must learn who made up the population, where people came from, what sorts of churches people supported, how many people were rich and how many poor, who went to school and who did not, what were the conditions of work, and so forth. The use of statistics can materially assist the historian in his search for information of this kind. Statistics, however, must be used with care and understanding, and it is the purpose of this appendix to pass along some of the experience of the author to others who wish to work in the field of local history.

The problems and potentialities of historical statistics will be discussed in three aspects: first, the area of study and the related problems of bound-aries; second, the reliability of census and other enumerations; third, sug-gestions for the construction of a statistical sketch for a small area.

THE AREA OF STUDY

Excepting the special case of some simplified political histories, the geographical areas of historical study only by accident coincide with those of the U. S. Census and other enumerations. The historian's districts are functional and conceptual. His area is the space which encompasses the forces and events he wishes to describe. For instance, his geographical bounds might be the area to which an immigrant group moved, the region of a religious sect, the district where a particular kind of farming or industry predominated, the *de facto* not the *de jure* boundaries of a city or town. The geographical units of the Census, of deeds, or of birth records, are either political—precincts, wards, towns, counties, and states—or, as in the case of the twentieth century Census, arbitrary: Census tracts arranged for the convenience of an enumerator's walking canvass.

A valley or the spur of a transcontinental railroad may constitute the functional unit for the historian of rural life. Neither district is likely to appear as a census unit, or to be a category in the published records of the railroad company. Similarly, the city limits of a rural market town may encompass a large farming population; or, as in the case of most American metropolitan cities, the limits may include but a fraction of the economic and social life of the city. Within cities themselves the wards and precincts, upon whose boundaries nineteenth century enumerations were based, more often reflect political compromises at the state legislature or City Hall than the functioning quarters of the city. Parishes, shopping habits, transportation paths, class divisions, and the work areas of the city were frequently jumbled together or arbitrarily split apart by municipal ward boundaries. Twentieth century Census tracts are an improvement over the ward since they are small in area, but their boundaries are frequently changed from Census to Census so that comparisons over time are difficult to make.

Because of this conflict of boundaries between the historian's conceptual district and the political boundaries of most statistical tabulations much of the statistical information used by the historian can be approximations only. Nor can there be a single method of adjustment which will bring all Census statistics into harmony since each Census differs from its predecessor and each therefore requires new methods of adjustment.

Intensive small-scale histories like studies of a parish, or a school, or a Grange, can escape the problems of boundaries by using the original Census schedules prepared by the individual enumerators. Such schedules still exist for all states from the time of their statehood on, with the exception of a few southern states during the years prior to the Civil War. The schedules, if examined by the historian of a parish or local organization, would go far in illustrating the relationship of an organization to the community that surrounded it. This dimension of history is now woefully presented in such fragmentary accounts as do exist. A descriptive guide to the original Census materials is provided by National Archives, *Guide to the Records in the National Archives* (Washington, 1948).

Whatever the local historian's choice of boundaries his work can be speeded by consulting Carroll D. Wright and William C. Hunt, *History and Growth of the U. S. Census, 1790–1890* (Washington, 1900). Wright and Hunt list the questions asked by the enumerators, discuss the methods of the Census, and give some rough estimates as to the reliability of each Census.

RELIABILITY OF ENUMERATIONS

Today's historical monograph literature demonstrates a very substantial interest in statistical documentation. This increasing use of statistical material derives in large measure from the increase in analytical presentations at the expense of the former narrative style histories. The twentieth century scholars' interest in social phenomena has given especially strong incentives for the use and interpretation of statistics from the past.

Often in recent monographs there has been an overuse of statistics and a too heavy reliance upon the accuracy of past enumerations. The concept of an enumeration—the physical counting of all the inhabitants and their property at one moment in time—is such a simple and attractive one that it has probably been misleading historians ever since Domesday Book. Until very recently American censuses have been like all enumerations before them. The municipal, state, and federal censuses have purported to be complete physical counts of all the relevant persons and objects within a given geographical area. The attempt to send out men to count everything gave rise to a variety of errors. For all but the most exhaustive statistical studies, however, the degree and direction of the past census errors are indeterminate because no measurements of enumeration accuracy were made at the time of the canvasses.

The method of old censuses of population, and many censuses of property as well, was to have an enumerator visit each dwelling in his district, and there inquire of the head of household the number of resident persons, their names, ages, occupations, places of birth, and so forth. If housing and property information was being sought the head of the household was to be the source for this material also. In the event that the enumerator could not find the residents of a dwelling at home, after several attempts, he was to inquire of the neighbors for as much information as they could supply. Economic statistics on working conditions, number and kinds of employees, number and value of products, and so forth, were collected by a combination of direct interviews with businessmen and farmers, the returns from mail questionnaires, and the use of published trade statistics.

Such enumeration methods provide a number of sources of error. It was a popular opinion among American heads of households that census takers were but tax collectors in diguise and this natural suspicion must have led to the withholding of information concerning the number of boarders, rents, personal property, dwelling size, value, and use. The dependence upon neighbors for information about uncontacted families must also have resulted in substantial errors.

In the case of business statistics the absence of good company records, the difference between company record keeping and census interests, one businessman's desire to puff up the success of his firm, another's desire to hide his assets, all these factors introduced a succession of departures from the real state of affairs. Both the mail questionnaire and the published trade statistics left the enumerators ignorant of those concerns not reporting.

Not only did the sources for the census give rise to many errors but the enumerators themselves introduced a number of distortions. Sparsely settled rural districts, shanty towns that surrounded nineteenth century cities, and overcrowded slums, all defied accurate enumeration.

How many errors and what kinds of mistakes did lazy and tired enumerators and unreliable sources introduce into the published tallies of a given district? In theoretical terms the amount of error and its direction are indeterminate because systematic measurement of the errors was not undertaken at the time of the census itself. Since 1940 the U. S. Census Bureau has followed its enumerators with random sample checks to discover the range of error of its enumerations. Until that time the Census Bureau relied upon the census supervisors' knowledge of local affairs to detect unreliable reports.

Common sense would suggest that the cumulative effect of laziness, transient elements in the population, and fear of taxation would together produce underreporting and therefore census errors would be negative in direction. It is not safe, however, to operate upon this assumption. Census enumerators were often paid by the number of persons they reported, and even conscientious enumerators when faced with crowded districts had to rely on secondhand information. In such cases they could, and did, make errors of overreporting as well as underreporting. Thus census users must be aware that any total they wish to use may be 100 percent accurate, or too large or too small, and unless the total can be checked against other sources they can never know the accuracy of an enumeration.

In the nineteenth century, Boston was much analyzed by state and local statisticians. It was also much taxed. As a result there survives from this period a relatively rich statistical literature. In some cases this literature afforded two or more separate enumerations of persons and dwellings within the same district. In no case did the city, state, and federal counts agree. The diversity among these enumerations varied from year to year and from subject to subject. Out of these comparisons the author developed a rule of thumb to approximate the range of errors in censuses. This rule was that no census figure should be taken as being more accurate than ±6 percent. In other words, if the census stated that 10,000 people lived in a given ward, the best guess that a historian could rely upon was that 9,400 to 10,600 people did in fact live there.

Professor Eric E. Lampard of the University of Wisconsin, a historian who has done a good deal of work with economic statistics, stated to the author that it was his experience that until cross checking had been done one should, on occasion, be prepared for errors in economic statistics of the range of ±10 percent. Two very useful discussions of error in the U. S. Census and the handling of both population and economic statistics are: Eric E. Lampard on agriculture, mining, and fishing statistics, in Harvey S. Perloff et al., *Regions, Resources, and Economic Growth* (Baltimore, 1960), pp. 611–620; and, for general discussion, Everett S. Lee et al., volume 1 of Simon Kuznets and Dorothy S. Thomas, *Population Redistribution and Economic Growth, United States, 1870–1950* (Philadelphia, 1957, 1960). I.

The presence of substantial errors in the census requires the local historian to use census data with the same sophistication he would use any other source. The past tendency to check writings of individuals against other sources but to accept statistics as prima facie fact must be abandoned. The presence or absence of particular kinds of churches or societies, information from real estate atlases, newspaper accounts, assessors lists—all such information can tell the historian how much reliance he should place upon a given set of statistics. Most of this cross-information will be non-numerical. The author's rule of thumb of ±6 percent is only an approximation and applies specifically to Boston material for the years 1870–1905. It is intended as a warning to others, not as a substitute for their own cross-checking and personal judgment.

The Statistical Sketch

For all the hazards of indeterminate errors and exasperating boundary changes census enumerations remain a vital source of information. If local historians are to write modern histories which can establish meaningful traditions for their communities they will have to rely upon statistical material to give them some of the general outlines of the common life of the past.

The traditional local history has concentrated upon the highly visible families, institutions, and industries, whether this material concerned the life of one thousandth or one half the population of the town. There have been two justifications for this course: first, that which was unique about a given town or county was generally the achievement of a small group of people; second, by and large, the wealthy and successful were the only people who left detailed records of their lives. As a result of his dependence upon literary sources the local historian has often become the prisoner of those families and institutions who preserved their records.

If in the course of his research the local historian would draw up a statistical sketch of his community he would to a certain extent release himself from the domination of literary evidence. At the same time such a sketch, no matter how rough, would provide him with a number of useful reference points by which he could orient his narrative. A reasonably satisfactory statistical sketch of any American community can be constructed for any time span subsequent to the Civil War. Such a sketch will not meet the standards of detail and accuracy required for contemporary sociological and economic analysis, but it will give useful approximations of past conditions.

The construction of a statistical sketch may be considered in two parts —those materials which tell of the numbers and movement of people, and those which tell of the environment within which the population lived.

In a rapidly growing, rapidly changing country like the United States, every historical study must consider the movement of population. Statistics of internal migration, however, are difficult to arrive at if the territorial unit chosen is smaller than a state. The exact number of people moving into a small area over a given period cannot be determined because Census materials only record net change at ten year intervals. All the local historian can do is look at the interstate figures on migration and be aware that for his community the amount of moving both interstate and intra-state may well have been far in excess or far less than what is suggested by the decennial changes in population. Simon Kuznets and Dorothy S. Thomas, *Population Redistribution and Economic Growth, United States, 1870–1950* (Philadelphia, 1957, 1960), 2 vols., is the basic modern study of the migration of the United States population. Everett S. Lee and Anne S. Lee, "Internal Migration Statistics for the U. S.," *Journal of the American Statistical Association,* 56:664–697 (Dec. 1960), is a summary of this study. The material is listed by state, and in this book and article there are excellent discussions of the problems of migration analysis and the accuracy of the Census.

Decennial enumerations of residents do yield statistics of the gross increase in population from one Census year to the next. This gross increase is an important figure in its own right, and it can be roughly adjusted to reflect the net immigration by removing the increment of natural increase in population caused by the excess of births over deaths. This adjustment of gross population change is especially important when studying periods and places of slow growth because one can easily in such cases mistake a stagnant situation for a modest boom when the natural increase is providing most of the population gain.

Unfortunately the correction factor for natural increase in population must be a vague guess. In the nineteenth century the United States birth rate was unmeasured and the death rate was not reported for all parts of the nation. Dr. J. S. Billings, a late nineteenth century authority on vital statistics, has published a discussion of the problems in this field and his estimate of the birth rate in U. S. Census, *Special Reports, Twelfth Census* (Washington, 1906), pp. 405–409. His educated guess is an excess of births over deaths of 0.5 to 1.0 percent per year for the second half of the nineteenth century. This figure could be used as a rough correction factor for this period. For a more complete and modern treatment of problems of natural increase, with up-to-date references, see Kuznets and Thomas, *Population Redistribution,* I, 1–56.

The general nature and geographic background of the population, whatever its moving patterns, can usually be easily determined by consulting published statistics. Both federal and local censuses frequently issued statistics of native and foreign born, white and Negro, men and women. Often detailed statistics were also assembled for the number of children of foreign born by the origin of their parents. Religious affiliations of the population are not as a rule available, although street directories and other sources give the number and denominations of churches, and the denominations themselves have published membership claims. Since the nineteenth and early twentieth century were periods of enormous foreign immigration the compilation of ethnic statistics is well worthwhile. In addition, note should be taken of cases in which males and females are out of the usual range for the region and period. Aberrations of this sort may give the historian a clue to a large concentration of domestics, a large bachelor working force, or the location and movement of temporary frontier conditions.

Age statistics, like those of internal migration, are generally published in satisfactory detail only for states. Such local breakdowns as exist are apt to distinguish only between the 20–65 age group and all others. Occasionally a school census or special study was undertaken which gave ages by five-year intervals. Such age statistics when used in conjunction with those of occupations could suggest varying patterns of child labor and education among the classes of a locality. They might also indicate some migration patterns within the locality by pointing to clusters of old people, children, and young adults. Unless good age details are ready at hand, however, it is the author's experience that age statistics do not yield results commensurate to the effort required to compile them. Both the population's false reporting of ages, and the changing grouping of age intervals, made these statistics such approximations that they could not be used as a basis for generalizations for social history.

The environmental material of a statistical sketch of a locality is best constructed by combining the statistical literature with direct observation of the features of the site and observation of the extant artifacts. For most localities frequent statistics exist for the number of dwellings, the occupations of the inhabitants, and the principal products and trade of the district. From the population and dwelling statistics one can prepare density lists: the number of people per house, per acre, per ward and so forth. Such figures give a good idea of the areas of growth in a county or city. If these density lists are examined and compared to similar lists of occupations and ethnic origin, a rough outline of the social and class patterns of the community will emerge.

The basic statistics of housing, density, and occupations can be supplemented by consulting registration data and special studies. Registration data—deeds, licenses, tax lists, marriage, birth, and death records—are familiar tools of the local historian. This sort of material exists in great abundance and is useful because it gives the names and addresses of individuals. Local historians will want to sample this material in order to establish a link between the general summary view of their census statistics and the biographical dimensions of their narratives. This registration data can also be used systematically to test generalizations. For instance, tax assessors' lists or real estate atlases can be tabulated by the ethnicity of the names to establish an approximate relationship between land tenure and national origin.

The kind and number of special statistical studies varies from place to place, but since the Civil War special studies of all sorts have been made by private and public investigators. Sanitary and drainage surveys often tell much about housing and living conditions. Street railway and railroad traffic analyses supplement occupational figures by placing more clearly the patterns of people's movement. Old mortgage and tenure statistics give further information on standards of living. Factory and tenement investigations are extremely useful because they often combine statistics with direct reporting. The statistics give the modern reader a good check on the quality of the reporting, and the reporting tells much more than the bare bones of the survey would indicate. If before consulting the occasional and special statistical literature the historian would construct a brief profile of his population he would then be in the best possible position to make good use of the fragments. Donald D. Parker, *Local History* (Social Science Research Council, Bertha E. Josephson, ed., rev. ed., New York, 1944), is a still useful guide to the sources of local history. For a convenient guide to urban material in all U. S. censuses see U. S. National Resources Committee, "Urban Government," *Supplementary Report of the Urbanism Subcommittee* (Washington, 1939), I, 162–174.

When a historian wishes to mix local, state, and federal statistics, or when his social and economic statistics span a period of time he is sure to confront the problem of varying definitions. Each study may make use of different definitions when counting roughly the same material. A census series may change its definition from decade to decade. On the other hand, the definition may remain constant over a long period of time but the object which it describes may vary sharply from the beginning to the end of a period. The tenement or the farm of 1850 is not the same creature as the tenement or the farm of 1900.

The first kind of definition problem concerns the use of different definitions by separate studies. For example, one census counts occupied dwellings; another, occupied and unoccupied dwellings; a third, dwelling units; a fourth, those structures whose use was primarily for dwelling purposes. Sometimes several different definitions are used at the same time by separate studies and in this case some measure of the variations among them can be determined. More often than not, no numerical comparison is possible and the decision of comparability must rest with the judgment of the historian.

The second, and perhaps most difficult definition problem, concerns the interpretation of old definitions. The study of occupations, like that of housing and family size, is often obscured by shifting definitions of what constituted manufacturing as a whole, what were the different types of manufacturing, and what were the proper definitions to describe the jobs within any given industry. For the local historian, a scholar not primarily concerned with gathering empirical data for the testing of an economic theory, the problem of definitions centers around the correct interpretation of each statistical study as a discrete description of its own period.

It is difficult to draw social generalization from a detailed occupational list that goes on for pages in units of: 4 chocolate makers, 7 curriers, 1 engraver, 2 morocco workers, 4 willow-ware makers, 1 horse shoer, and so forth. On the other hand, old general categories like "at home," "laborer," "clerk," "mechanic," and so forth, cover so many conditions of life that it is hard to know what might lie beneath the general categories.

These problems of definition, like the problem of the errors in the enumerations, require the local historian to regard his statistical material as an assembly of crude fragments out of which he must build his story in the same manner as any writer must. The statistical fragments, however carefully constructed, are an assembly to which only the historian's imagination can bring order.

It has been the experience of the author that consulting old maps, drawings, and photographs, and above all walking about in the sections of the city where the artifacts of the period still stand, or once stood, are the most useful ways to cultivate the historical imagination necessary to order the fragments of the library and museum. To see the old factory, the old farm, or the old neighborhood is an experience which more than any other can give the historian the point of view necessary to interpret his library fragments and can call his attention to dimensions of past life which he may have neglected or have as yet been unable to discover.

APPENDIX B

TABLES

TABLE 1. Location of metropolitan population, 1850 and 1900*

Location	1850		1900	
	Inhabitants	Percent	Inhabitants	Percent
Living in the pedestrian city, two-mile radius: Boston, Roxbury, Cambridge, and Charlestown	187,676	66.6	504,553	44.2
Living in the peripheral towns of the early railroad and omnibus era. Two- to three-mile radius: Brookline, Chelsea, Dorchester, and Somerville	20,726	7.3	195,349	17.1
Subtotal. Pre-streetcar metropolis, three-mile radius	208,402	73.9	699,902	61.3
Living in the new suburbs, railroad and streetcar commuters. Three- to ten-mile radius: Quincy to Lynn	73,664	26.1	441,642	38.7
Total, ten-mile metropolis	282,066	100.0	1,141,544	100.0

* Due to the irregularities of town boundaries this table shows approximate shifts in population only. Especially the growth of the peripheral towns is overstated since all these towns but Chelsea had boundaries that stretched from two to five miles from Boston's City Hall.

Source: J. D. B. DeBow, *Seventh Census* (Washington, 1853), pp. 50–52; U. S. Census Office, *Twelfth Census* (Washington, 1901), I, 198–201.

TABLE 2. Population in the study area,* 1870–1905

		Gain	
Year	Population	Number	Percent
1870	59,519		
1875	83,329	23,810	40.0
1880	95,691	12,362	14.8
1885	111,941	16,250	16.9
1890	144,927	32,986	29.5
1895	181,099	36,172	25.0
1900	227,431	46,332	25.6
1905	251,738	24,307	10.7

* The study area is defined as the 1875–1895 wards of the City of Boston which together included most of the area of the three former towns. There were some differences between the old town boundaries and these ward boundaries. For this reason 6.83 percent has been added to the 1870 and 1875 census tabulations; these listings are thus comparable to the ward boundaries adopted November 10, 1875. The ward boundaries changed again in 1895 but the total effect on the study area was so small that the census figures have been left unchanged. It is estimated that the census figures overstate the population by .08 percent in 1895 and by 1.09 percent in 1900. The error for 1905 is indeterminate.

Source: Mass. and U. S. Censuses.

TABLE 3. Population of the study area as a percentage of Boston's population, and its gain in relation to Boston's gain

Year	Percentage of Boston's population	Study area's gain as percentage of Boston's gain
1870	20.3*	
1875	24.4	48.2
1880	26.4	59.1
1885	28.7	59.0
1890	32.3	56.8
1895	36.4	74.7
1900	40.5	72.4
1905	42.3	70.5

* 41,973 was added to Boston's population for Charlestown, Brighton, and West Roxbury which were not yet annexed.

Sources: *Ninth Census*, I, 167, 646; *Mass. Census, 1875*, I, 5, 7; *Tenth Census*, I, 670; Carroll D. Wright, *Social Statistics*, pp. 12, 13; *Mass. Census, 1885*, I, 5–7; *Eleventh Census*, I, 460–461; *Mass. Census, 1895*, IV, 76, 118; *Twelfth Census*, I, 620; II, 124–125; *Mass. Census, 1905*, I, 662, 665.

TABLE 4. Population, families, and dwellings* in the study area, 1870–1905

Year	Population	Number of families	Persons per family	Number of dwellings	Persons per dwelling	Families per dwelling	Number of new dwellings	Percent increase in dwellings
1870	59,519	12,297	4.84	8,545	6.97	1.44	—	—
1875	83,329	17,453	4.77	11,494	7.25	1.52	2,949	34.5
1880	95,691	19,540	4.90	13,448	7.12	1.45	1,954	17.0
1885	111,941	23,398	4.78	14,924	8.00	1.57	1,476	11.0
1890	144,927	30,437	4.76	19,584	7.40	1.55	4,660	31.2
1895	181,099	39,531	4.58	24,507	7.39	1.61	4,923	25.1
1900	227,431	50,243	4.53	31,059	7.32	1.62	6,552	26.7
1905	251,738	56,781	4.43	—	—	—	—	—

* The definition of a dwelling is in all cases a dwelling house, a structure; it is not a dwelling unit, a room or series of rooms in a structure. See *Mass. Census, 1895*, I, 795; Carroll D. Wright, *Social Statistics*, p. 10; *Twelfth Census*, II, clvi, 614; and *Historical Statistics of the U. S.*, pp. 164–166.

Sources: 1870: *Ninth Census*, I, 598–599; 1875: *Mass. Census, 1875*, I, 22–23; 1880: Carroll D. Wright, *Social Statistics*, p. 14 and *Tenth Census*, I, 670; 1885: *Mass. Census, 1885*, I, 167, 172–174; 1890: *Eleventh Census*, I, 913, 936, 956; 1895: *Mass. Census, 1895*, I, 760–777; 1900: *Twelfth Census*, II, 614, 645–646; 1905: *Mass. Census, 1905*, I, 662, 665.

TABLE 5. Number of foreign born by nation in inner wards (Roxbury) and outer wards (Dorchester and West Roxbury), 1875–1890

	1875*		1880		1890	
	Inner	Outer	Inner	Outer	Inner	Outer
Canada	2,254	1,329	3,253	1,590	8,622	4,203
Great Britain	2,197	884	2,272	967	3,794	2,030
Ireland	10,397	4,231	10,909	4,348	14,821	4,747
Germany	2,509	664	2,571	694	3,298	1,155
Russia	27	7	57	1	303	81
Others	801	244	1,091	288	2,375	1,199
Totals	18,185	7,359	20,153	7,888	33,213	13,415
Percentage distribution of each nationality group						
Canada	62.9	37.1	67.2	32.8	67.2	32.8
Great Britain	71.3	28.7	70.2	29.8	65.3	34.7
Ireland	71.1	28.9	71.5	28.5	75.7	24.3
Germany	79.1	20.9	78.7	21.3	74.1	25.9
Russia	79.4	20.6	98.3	1.7	79.0	21.0
Others	76.7	23.3	79.1	20.9	66.4	33.6
All Groups	71.2	28.8	71.9	28.1	71.2	28.8

* The ward boundaries of 1875 were different from those of 1880 and 1890. There is no reliable way to compensate for this change.

Source: *Mass. Census, 1875,* I, 279–282, 287–339; Carroll D. Wright, *Social Statistics,* pp. 16–43; *Tenth Census,* I, 538–539. The statistics of 1890 are taken from the only available source which gave ward breakdowns, the "Tenement House Census of 1891." The figures are a projection of the proportions of foreign born among house renters; house renters constituted at that time about 65 percent of the population. Mass. Bureau of the Statistics of Labor, Twenty-second Annual Report, *Public Document No. 15,* (Boston, 1892), pp. 524–527, 539.

TABLE 6. Estimate of dwellings by types in the study area, 1870–1900

Year	Total dwellings	Single-family		Two-family		Three-family		More than three families	
		Number	Percentage of total	Number	Percentage of total	Number	Percentage of total	Number	Percentage of total
1870	8,545	6,528	76.4	1,418	16.6	300	3.5	299	3.5
1875	11,494	—	—	—	—	—	—	—	—
1880	13,448	9,535	70.9	2,542	18.9	968	7.2	403*	3.0
1885	14,924	—	—	—	—	—	—	—	—
1890	19,584	12,800	65.4	4,145	21.2	2,026	10.3	613*	3.1
1895	24,507	14,996	61.2	5,402	22.0	3,480	14.2	629*	2.6
1900	31,059	18,594	59.9	7,294	23.5	4,469	14.4	702	2.2

* The U. S. and Mass. Censuses give the number of dwellings by type only for the years 1890, 1895, 1900; earlier only the total of all dwelling structures were listed. This estimate is a projection of conditions and changes in the last decade back upon the earlier years. The figures given seem reasonable and reflect the big boom in three-deckers after 1885. The category "more than three families," which was a residual one, is patently in error. It contradicts both old assessors records and present day observations. An educated guess would be that for all years this category ranged between 2 and 5 percent of the total structures.

TABLE 7. Four types of builders, classified by the size of their operations,* and their contribution to new dwelling construction, study area, 1872–1901

Type of builder	Number of builders	Number of dwellings	Percent of total dwellings	Group average (dwellings per builder)
Those who built twenty or more dwellings over the whole period	122	5,350	23.0	43.85
Those who built five or more dwellings in some one year, but less than twenty in the whole period	279	2,498	11.0	8.95
Those who built two to four dwellings in some one year, but less than twenty in the whole period	1,949	7,542	32.7	3.87
Those who built no more than one dwelling in any one year, and less than twenty in the whole period	6,680	7,683	33.3	1.15
Total	9,030	23,073	100.0	—

* This classification of builders by the number of dwellings they decided to build in their most active year of construction was imposed by the necessity of one man's classifying 28,000 separate building permits. Though peculiar categories in some ways they have the merit of giving results based on all builders' behavior.

TABLE 8. Comparison of the random sample of 361 builders and the 122 most active builders, occupation and place of residence, 1872–1901

	The 361				The 122			
Occupation	Number	Percentage of group	Number of dwellings	Percentage of dwellings	Number	Percentage of group	Number of dwellings	Percentage of dwellings
Agriculture and fishing	7	1.9	8	0.9	none	—	—	—
Manufacturing	15	4.2	34	4.0	3	2.5	99	1.8
Building and construction	111	30.1	336	39.3	87	71.3	3753	70.1
Transport	17	4.7	26	3.0	3	2.5	116	2.2
Trade	83	23.0	157	18.4	14	11.5	507	9.5
Public service	4	1.1	5	0.6	none	—	—	—
Professional	17	4.7	45	5.3	7	5.7	422	7.9
Domestic and personal	2	0.6	2	0.2	1	0.8	30	0.6
Unknown and unattached	105	29.1	242	28.3	7	5.7	423	7.9
Totals	361	99.3	855	100.0	122	100.0	5350	100.0

Place of Residence*								
Within 2 blocks of most of his building	89	24.7				40.2		
Within one-half mile of most of his building	57	15.8				14.5		
In the study area	59	16.3				18.0		
Total in study area or closer	205	56.8				72.7		
In Central Boston	38	10.5				11.2		
Elsewhere in Massachusetts	12	3.3				8.4		
Address unknown	106	29.4				7.5		
Totals	361	100.0				100.0		

* For the 361 builders this tabulation is based on a comparison of the address of a builder at the moment he took out his first building permit with the addresses of the majority of the structures he put up over the entire thirty year period of study. Source for addresses was the Boston Street Directory. The 122 builders were studied in a more detailed way. As a result only proportional comparisons can be made between the two groups.

BIBLIOGRAPHICAL NOTE

THE GENERAL BACKGROUND

Since 1941 the history of Boston has been steadily rewritten. The new school of thought was largely begun by Oscar Handlin, whose *Boston's Immigrants* appeared in that year. A number of books, of which the present one is but the latest, have taken up different aspects of the city's history from the new point of view. These include:

Handlin, Oscar, *Boston's Immigrants,* Cambridge, 1941; rev. ed., 1959.

Firey, Walter, *Land Use in Central Boston,* Cambridge, 1947.

Mann, Arthur, *Yankee Reformers in the Urban Age,* Cambridge, 1954.

Solomon, Barbara M., *Ancestors and Immigrants,* Cambridge, 1956.

Blake, John B., *Public Health in the Town of Boston 1630–1822,* Cambridge, 1959.

Huthmacher, J. Joseph, *Massachusetts People and Politics,* Cambridge, 1959.

Rodwin, Lloyd, *Housing and Economic Progress,* Cambridge, 1961.

For those readers who wish to pursue some of the topics covered in this book the following books and articles are recommended.

ANNEXATION

Chandler, Alfred D., *Annexation of Brookline to Boston,* Brookline, 1880.

Choate, Rufus, *Speech on the Application of Samuel D. Bradford and Others To Set Off Wards 6, 7, & 8 of the City of Roxbury as a Separate Agricultural Town,* Boston, 1851.

Clifford, John H., *Argument on the Question of the Annexation of Roxbury to Boston before the Legislative Committee, Thursday, February 23, 1865,* Boston, 1867.

Harris, B. W., *The Annexation Question, Closing Argument for the Remonstrants against the Annexation of Dorchester to Boston . . . ,* Boston, 1869.

McCaffrey, George H., "Political Disintegration and Reintegration of Metropolitan Boston," unpubl. diss., 1937. Typescript in the Harvard College Library, Cambridge.

Roxbury Committee opposed to the Annexation to Boston, *A Word for Old Roxbury,* Roxbury, 1851.

188 | BIBLIOGRAPHICAL NOTE

Hitchcock, Henry-Russell, *Architecture, Nineteenth and Twentieth Centuries,* Baltimore, 1958.
———— *A Guide to Boston Architecture, 1637–1954,* New York, 1954.
Kilham, Walter H., *Boston After Bulfinch,* Cambridge, 1946.
Mumford, Lewis, *Sticks and Stones,* 2nd. rev. ed., New York, 1955.
Scully, Vincent J., Jr., *The Shingle Style,* New Haven, 1955.
Whitehill, Walter M., *Boston: A Topographical History,* Cambridge, 1959.

BOSTON

Bacon, Edwin M., *Walks and Rides in the Country round about Boston,* Cambridge, 1898.
Herlihy, Elisabeth M., ed., *Fifty Years of Boston,* Boston, 1932.
Huse, Charles P., *The Financial History of Boston from May 1, 1822 to January 31, 1909,* Cambridge, 1916.
Lord, Robert L., John E. Sexton, and Edward T. Harrington, *History of the Archdiocese of Boston, 1604–1943,* 3 vols., New York, 1944.
Matthews, Nathan, Jr., *The City Government of Boston,* Boston, 1895.
McNamara, Katherine, *The Boston Metropolitan District: A Bibliography,* Cambridge, 1946.
Winsor, Justin, ed., *The Memorial History of Boston,* 4 vols., Boston, 1881–1886.
Woods, Robert A., ed., *The City Wilderness,* Boston, 1898.
———— ed., *Americans In Process,* Boston, 1903.

HOUSING

Hale, Edward E., *Workingmen's Homes,* Boston, 1879.
Massachusetts Bureau of Statistics of Labor, "Tenement House Census," *Twenty-second and Twenty-third Annual Reports, Public Document no. 15.,* 2 vols., Boston, 1892–1893.
Paine, Robert Treat, "Homes for the People," *Journal of Social Science,* 15:1–19 (Sept. 1881).
———— "Housing Conditions of Boston," *Annals of the American Academy of Political and Social Science,* 3:121–136 (July 1902).
U. S. Works Progress Administration, *Real Property Inventory of Boston,* 2 vols., Multilith, Boston, 1934–1936.
Wolfe, Albert B., *The Lodging House Problem in Boston,* Cambridge, 1913.

LOCAL HISTORIES

Barrows, Rev. Samuel J., "Dorchester 1870–1899," typescript, c. 1900, in the Dorchester Historical Society.
Drake, Francis S., *The Town of Roxbury,* Roxbury, 1878.
Orcutt, William D., *Good Old Dorchester, 1630–1893,* Cambridge, 1893.
Simonds, Thomas J., *History of South Boston,* Boston, 1857.
Sumner, William H., *A History of East Boston,* Boston, 1858.
Woods, Robert A., and Albert J. Kennedy, *The Zone of Emergence* (Sam B. Warner, Jr., ed.). Cambridge, 1962.

PARKS

Boston Board of Park Commissioners, *Second Report of 1876, City Document no. 42,* Boston, 1876.

Crafts, William A., *Forest Hills Cemetery,* Roxbury, 1855.

Dearborn, Nathaniel, *Guide Through Mount Auburn,* 8th ed., Boston, 1854.

Eliot, Charles, *A Report on the Opportunities for Parks and Open Spaces in the Metropolitan District of Boston Presented to the Metropolitan Park Commission,* Boston, 1893.

Olmsted, Frederick Law, *Notes on the Plan of Franklin Park,* Boston, 1886.

PUBLIC HEALTH

Whipple, George C., *State Sanitation, A Review of the Work of the Massachusetts Board of Health,* 2 vols., Cambridge, 1917.

SCHOOLS

Boston School Committee, *Annual Reports 1900–1903,* 3 vols., Boston, 1901–1904.

Hale, Richard W., Jr., *Tercentenary History of the Roxbury Latin School, 1645–1945,* Cambridge, 1946.

TRANSPORTATION

A. B. C. Pathfinder Railway Guide, monthly, Boston, 1872–1901.

The Boston Directory, 34 vols., Boston, 1871–1903.

"Boston Elevated and West End Street Railway, Historical Dates Since January 2, 1892," typescript in the Library of the Boston Elevated Railway, Metropolitan Transit Authority Office, Boston.

Hager, Louis P., *History of the West End Street Railway,* Boston, 1892.

Mason, Edward S., *The Street Railway in Massachusetts,* Cambridge, 1932.

The Detailed Search

The building of a city is such a piecemeal process that except for a few of the architecturally most notable buildings no ordinary historical record survives. To discover who built the three towns of Roxbury, West Roxbury, and Dorchester one must put together a variety of legal records and published sources, each one of which was intended for a purpose other than subsequent historical analysis. Perhaps if the steps taken for the research for this book were described briefly here the local historian's interest might be aroused and his curiosity armed with some hints as to what questions can be asked of what materials.

who were the decision makers?

The building permits of the City of Boston give the name of the owner of the land at the time an application to build a house was made. These records consist of large bound volumes whose first entry is October 1, 1871.

The permits list as well the ground floor area of the structure; the number of stories; the material of construction; the name of the contractor; the approximate address and, from 1899 on, the name of the architect, if any; and the number of families for which the house was intended.

For the three former towns of Roxbury, West Roxbury, and Dorchester during the years 1872–1901 approximately 28,000 building permits were issued. By sampling the entire list of builders and checking the occupations and addresses of the random sample against the listings in the Street Directory some idea of occupation, moving patterns, and purpose of building could be inferred. Biographical information came by a variety of routes. The index to the obituaries of the *Boston Evening Transcript* yeilded the most; old biographical volumes told of a few more; the lists of family names and family histories in the library of the New England Historic Genealogical Society provided some excellent material; finally, a list of names was sent to the Dorchester Historical Society and to all the real estate men of the three towns—their memories turned up a few more leads. Biographical sketches of two dozen builders are given in the author's "The Residential Development of Roxbury, West Roxbury, and Dorchester, Massachusetts, 1870–1900," unpubl. diss., Harvard University, 1959.

WHAT DID THEY BUILD?

The contemporary real estate atlases were extremely useful in this study for checking results of the building permit analysis. For those wishing to do limited studies they perhaps would be the place to begin. In Boston there are two atlas series. G. Morgan Hopkins, *Atlas of the County of Suffolk, Massachusetts* (Philadelphia, 1873–4), 7 volumes; and George W. and Walter S. Bromley, *Atlas of the City of Boston* (Philadelphia, 1883–1928), 7 volumes with frequent revisions. These atlases give the name of the owner of each parcel of land, the outlines of his lot and house, the number of square feet of area in the lot, the material of the structures, the location of the water lines, and some of the sewer lines. Because they were issued frequently these atlases provide a running history of the location of new houses and the rough timing of the arrival of municipal services.

For a detailed history of an individual house or subdivision, its financing and legal restrictions, there is no recourse but to disappear into that organized morass, the Registry of Deeds. Armed with the name of the owner of the land at any moment of time, one may trace the property backwards or forwards through the records. A giant index of hundreds of volumes for the years 1630–1899 guides one from the man granting away the title to his property to the man who received it, and under each name is a listing of the volume and page of the record book into which the legal instrument of the transaction was copied. Subdivision plans accompany many deeds and can be found bound with them. For studies of single houses and small areas no source can match the deeds for usefulness. For the study of a large district, as in this book, they can only be sampled.

Finally, walking about the three towns proved to be the best way to assemble the parts of the detailed research, and the best way to gain new insights. The buildings themselves, their ornament and their placement on the site proved the ultimate test of scholarly detective work.

WHO MOVED IN?

In cases where the builder moved into his own house the biographical research on the background of builders could be used to answer the question of occupancy. In addition the Massachusetts and United States Censuses gave some general social and economic information. There were errors in the censuses, categories changed from year to year, and shifting boundaries of census districts caused further problems. For more discussion of this subject the reader is referred to Appendix A. The tables of statistics themselves are in the author's "Residential Development of Roxbury, West Roxbury, and Dorchester, Massachusetts, 1870–1900," unpubl. diss., Harvard University, 1959. This study contains a 108-page appendix with fifty tables, and is accompanied by a separate atlas showing the location of transportation and new house construction. The statistics include tables for the three towns taken as a whole, ward divisions where possible, comparisons between the three towns and Boston as a whole, and comparisons between the three towns and the nearby suburban city of Cambridge. Scholars may consult this material in the Harvard Library, or write the author to arrange for microfilm copies.

NOTES

CHAPTER ONE. A CITY DIVIDED

1. For an introduction to the problems of the literature on hours, wages, and cost of living: U. S. Bureau of the Census, *Historical Statistics of the United States, 1789–1945* (Washington, 1949), pp. 56–59; the sociology of American capitalism: John E. Sawyer, "The Entrepreneur and the Social Order," *Men in Business,* ed. William Miller (Cambridge, 1952), pp. 6–22; for the local versions of the middle class ideology see Sam B. Warner, Jr., "The Residential Development of Roxbury, West Roxbury, and Dorchester, Massachusetts, 1870–1900" (unpubl. diss., Harvard University, 1959), pp. 60–64.

2. In the late nineteenth century, a period of enormous immigration, students tended to confuse immigrant attitudes with lower class attitudes. The outlines of a lower class group without middle class aspirations can, however, be perceived even in Bushee's prejudiced study. Its presence can be inferred from his difficulties in explaining the high rate of pauperism among natives and the "old immigration." Frederick A. Bushee, "Ethnic Factors in the Population of Boston," *Publications of the American Economic Association* (Third Series, New York, 1903), 4:12–37, 84–97, 149–161. A more perceptive analysis is Albert J. Kennedy's chapter on Roxbury Crossing in Robert A. Woods and Albert J. Kennedy, eds., "The Zone of Emergence" (c. 1912; manuscript on deposit at the South End House, 20 Union Park street, Boston).

3. This estimate of the class divisions of Boston society probably is accurate within 10 percent. Also, during the last third of the nineteenth century middle class real income and the proportion of the middle class to total population increased somewhat. The estimates given in the text are those of the high 1900 levels; in 1870 the working class constituted 60 percent of the population. For a full discussion of the relationship of income to housing, and estimates as to the historical distribution of income, see Lloyd Rodwin, "Middle Income Housing Problems in Boston" (unpubl. diss., Harvard University, 1949), pp. 48–52, 77–82. This material was later published in *Housing and Economic Progress* (Cambridge, 1961).

CHAPTER TWO. THE LARGE INSTITUTIONS

1. At the time of writing Professor Charles J. Kennedy of the University of Nebraska was about to publish his history of the Boston and Maine Railroad. This book will contain a complete discussion of the early steam railroad and its associated commuting

patterns. I am indebted to Professor Kennedy for a citation of *Hunt's Merchant Magazine* (December 25, 1851, p. 759), which published a one-day traffic count of Boston. This count showed three equally popular means of entering and leaving the city: walking, riding the railroad, and traveling by carriage or omnibus.

2. The common mid-century South End land plan located single-family row houses on the side streets and mixed these row houses with tenement and store combinations on the main traffic streets. Tremont and Washington streets and Columbus, Shawmut, and Harrison avenues offered some moderately priced small rental units before the wholesale conversion of the single-family houses. Walter Muir Whitehill, *Boston: A Topographical History* (Cambridge, 1959), pp. 119–140; Suffolk Deeds, Liber 626, plan at end.

3. The original South Boston grid was broken in 1822 when narrow alleys were built behind the main streets. The alley lots were sold off for workers' housing. The resulting cramped land plan has provided a source of discomfort for 140 years. These alleys turn up in Harold K. Estabrook, *Some Slums in Boston* (Boston, 1898), pp. 21–23. Some alleys of houses have been replaced by federal housing projects; others still can be seen—for example, West 4th and 5th streets between E and F, and Silver and Gold streets. For the development of South Boston: Thomas C. Simonds, *History of South Boston* (Boston, 1857), pp. 72–104, 194–204, 300–313.

4. William H. Sumner, *A History of East Boston* (Boston, 1858), pp. 421–471; Suffolk Deeds, L. 401, end; Francis S. Drake, *The Town of Roxbury* (Roxbury, 1878), pp. 397–441; Woods and Kennedy, "The Zone of Emergence," chapters on Charlestown, South Boston, East Boston, Cambridgeport, East Cambridge, and Roxbury.

5. Good examples of the popular varieties of pre-streetcar city housing may be seen in Boston proper at Porter street; and in the lower South End, the blocks from Castle street to Worcester Square between Harrison avenue and Tremont street. Examples of the cheaper styles of the peripheral towns: in East Boston at Saratoga, Princeton, Lexington, and Trenton streets, between Marion and Brooks; in South Boston on West 4th and 5th streets; in Roxbury from Madison to Vernon streets between Tremont and Washington street; in Charlestown from Chelsea street to the Bunker Hill Monument; in East Cambridge, 3rd to 5th streets between Cambridge and Charles street.

6. Prentiss Cummings, "Street Railways of Boston," *Professional and Industrial History of Suffolk County, Mass.* (Boston, 1894), III, 289–290; Richard Herndon, *Boston of Today* (Boston, 1892), pp. 310–311; *Boston Evening Transcript,* November 24, 1882, editorial, p. 4; Robert H. Whitten, *Public Administration in Massachusetts* (New York, 1898), pp. 112–126.

7. Roswell F. Phelps, *South End Factory Operatives, Employment and Residence* (Boston, 1903), pp. 18–19.

8. For further discussion of tenure, see Warner, "Residential Development," Appendix D.

9. The street railwayman's credo: Henry M. Whitney and Prentiss Cummings, *Additional Burdens upon the Street Railway Companies, etc.* (Boston, 1891); the critics: *Citizen's Association of Boston Explaining Its Position. Statement of the Executive Committee Regarding . . . the Franchise Bill* (Boston, 1891).

10. The foregoing economic analysis of street railways is taken from Edward S. Mason, *The Street Railway in Massachusetts* (Cambridge, 1932), pp. 1–7, 71–113, 118–121. For detailed maps of street railway service see Warner, "Residential Development," Appendix E and Atlas.

11. George C. Whipple, *State Sanitation, A Review of the Work of the Massachusetts Board of Health* (Cambridge, 1917), II, 26–45; "Report on the Social Statistics of Cities," *Tenth Census* (Washington, 1887), XVIII, 106–162; Sam B. Warner, Jr., "Public Health Reform and the Depression of 1873–1878," *Bulletin of the History of Medicine*, 29:503–516 (Nov.-Dec. 1955); U. S. House of Representatives, 43rd Congress, 2nd Session, *Executive Document no. 95, The Cholera Epidemic of 1873* (Washington, 1875), pp. 563–682.

12. General Boston sanitary conditions before and after the public health movement can be studied by comparing Lemuel Shattuck, *Census of Boston for the Year 1845* (Boston, 1846), esp. pp. 56–57, with the Massachusetts Bureau of Statistics of Labor, *Twenty-third Annual Report, Massachusetts Public Document no. 15* (Boston, 1893), pp. 116–165. Approximate street by street conditions can be followed by consulting the real estate atlas series, George W. and Walter S. Bromley, *Atlas of the City of Boston* (Philadelphia, various editions from the first in 1883).

13. Robert H. Whitten, *Public Administration*, pp. 127–137; Frank P. Bennett, publ., *Bay State Gas* (Boston, 1899); E. M. Richards, *Is Municipal Ownership of Gas and Electric Lighting Desirable for Boston?* (Boston, 1905). The slow suburbanization of the telephone can be followed from the telephone listings in the Street Directory.

14. Uniformity of utility rates for a given class of customers was one of the important issues of the late nineteenth century, and its achievement was hampered by the divided and warring utility companies that served the Boston region. Louis D. Brandeis, *Consolidation of Gas Companies and of Electric Light Companies* (Boston, 1905).

15. Massachusetts Bureau of Statistics of Labor, *Third Annual Report, 1872, Senate Document no. 180* (Boston, 1873), p. 437; Dwight Porter, *Report upon a Sanitary Inspection of Certain Tenement-House Districts of Boston* (Boston, 1899); Estabrook, *Some Slums in Boston* (Boston, 1898).

16. During the years 1870–1900 the City of Boston built fifty-four primary and three high schools in the suburban towns of Roxbury, West Roxbury, and Dorchester. Boston School Committee, *Annual Report, 1870* (Boston, 1871), Appendix; *Annual Report, 1901* (Boston, 1902), pp. 220–224; *Annual Report 1902* (Boston, 1903), pp. 67–95.

17. Able summary by a conservative mayor of the role of municipal government: Nathan Matthews, Jr., *The City Government of Boston* (Boston, 1895), espec. pp. 104–107, 174–185; a reformer's beginning view that government may have to enter the field of housing for the poor: Francis A. Walker, "Introduction," in Porter, *Sanitary Inspection*, pp. v–vi; Estabrook, *Some Slums in Boston*, pp. 3–5, 21–23, opposed government intervention; Mayor Josiah Quincy, *The Development of American Cities* (reprinted from the *Arena*, Boston, March, 1897) was undecided about the role of government in housing.

18. Robert T. Paine, "The Housing Conditions of Boston," *Annals of the American Academy of Political and Social Science*, 3:124 (July 1902); Adna F. Weber, *The Growth of Cities in the Nineteenth Century* (New York, 1899), chap. 9; Woods and Kennedy, "The Zone of Emergence," introduction and chapter on Dorchester; Andrew J. Peters, "The City's Obligation in Housing," *Housing Problems in America* (New York, 1919), VII, 329–331.

19. The potential for an increase in lot sizes came with the great enlargement of the area occupied by the residences of metropolitan Boston. A survey of Bromley, *Atlas of Boston*, shows at least a doubling of lot sizes in all price ranges.

In the 1820's the Beacon Hill house covered 75 percent of its 1,500–2,300 square foot lot. In the 1830's the East Boston house used 50 percent of a 2,500 square foot lot. The South End houses of the 1850's used 50 percent of a 2,000–2,300 square foot lot. The expensive Back Bay house of the 1860's to 1890's covered two thirds of a 2,300–2,600 square foot lot. Cheap intown row houses and tenements of the pre-streetcar era were squeezed onto small lots that ranged from 600 to 1,400 square feet and covered 80–90 percent of the land.

The railroad commuter's "cottage" of the 1840's and 1850's commonly was placed on a square lot of 5,000 square feet. In the 1880's and 1890's the suburban lot sizes were enlarged from former city standards to the following approximate dimensions: three-deckers and cheap doubles and singles were placed on 2,400–2,700 square foot lots. The three-decker and the double used 50 percent of the lot, the single perhaps 30 percent. Moderately priced doubles had lots of 4,000–4,500 square feet and covered 25–30 percent of their land. A moderately priced single commonly had more land, 4,500–6,000 square feet, and occupied 20–30 percent of its lot.

CHAPTER THREE. THE THREE TOWNS

1. Approximate land areas of the three towns and Boston: Carroll D. Wright, *Social, Commercial, and Manufacturing Statistics of the City of Boston* (Boston, 1882), p. 6.

2. *Ninth Census*, I, 167; *Twelfth Census*, I, 630; comment on metropolitan rates of growth: U. S. Bureau of the Census, "Supplementary Analysis and Derivative Tables," *Special Reports, Twelfth Census* (Washington, 1906), pp. 51–54.

3. Rev. Samuel J. Barrows, "Dorchester 1870–1899" (MS, c.1900, at the Dorchester Historical Association, Boston Street, Dorchester, Mass.), p. 5.

CHAPTER FOUR. A SELECTIVE MELTING POT

1. Pre-1870 location of the central middle class: Whitehill, *A Topographical History*, pp. 95–140. For the houses standing in 1873–4 and the location of all new structures on maps of five year intervals from 1872–1901 see Warner, "Residential Development," Atlas.

2. Albert B. Wolfe, *The Lodging House Problem in Boston* (Cambridge, 1913), pp. 86–108; Phelps, *South End Factory Operatives*.

3. For further discussion of prices see Warner, "Residential Development," Appendix D; Phelps, *South End Factory Operatives*, pp. 40–41.

4. Because the number of upper middle class railroad commuters was small, their influence upon the total number of structures built in the suburbs was necessarily small. In a mass surburb of streetcar riders the upper middle class transportation and building patterns were buried under those of the majority groups. Upper middle class patterns stand out more clearly in a small town of railroad commuters like Dedham. Its population in 1850 was 4,447; in 1900, 7,457. When such small numbers were ranked against increases of 10,000 and more, an increase which was common to inner streetcar districts, the railroad contribution was buried. In districts other than the southern metropolitan sector of Roxbury, West Roxbury, and Dorchester the railroad may have played a more important role. The case of Newton is suggestive; it grew from 5,258 in 1850 to 33,587 in 1900. *Seventh Census*, pp. 50–52; *Twelfth Census*, I, 198–201.

5. Cheever Newhall, speculator and father of an even more active suburban builder, helped to establish the short-lived Dorchester Street Railway (1858–1863); Henry L. Pierce, land speculator, president of the Baker Chocolate Company, and mayor of

Boston, promoted the Dorchester Extension Railroad (1859–1863). The successful Highland Street Railway was created by citizens of Roxbury who lived in the fast-growing subdivisions off Warren street. Louis P. Hager, *History of the West End Street Railway* (Boston, 1892), pp. 18–19; Herndon, *Boston of Today*, pp. 310–311; *Boston Transcript*, November 24, 1882, editorial, p. 4; Sunday traffic: Frank Rowsome, Jr., *Trolley Car Treasury* (New York, 1956), pp. 95–104.

6. The progress of municipal services can be followed in Bromley, *Atlas of Boston*. The statutory framework: Henry E. Foley, *Special Laws of the Commonwealth of Massachusetts Relating to the City of Boston* (Boston, 1938), I, 86, 96, 164, 314, 392; Matthews, *The City Government of Boston*, pp. 59–66, 82–103; the City of Boston, *Revised Ordinances of 1892* (Boston, 1892), pp. 74–77. The dating of streets: Boston Street Commissioners, *A Record of the Streets, Alleys, Places, etc., in the City of Boston* (Boston, 1910), by street name. General survey of services: Charles P. Huse, *The Financial History of Boston* (Cambridge, 1916), by subject.

7. For rents, occupations, and ethnic distribution in the three towns see statistical tables in Warner, "Residential Development," Appendices A and B.

CHAPTER FIVE. THE WEAVE OF SMALL PATTERNS

1. Homer Hoyt, *Structure and Growth of Residential Neighborhoods in American Cities* (Washington, 1939), pp. 72–78, 112–122, 158; Robert E. Park, Ernest W. Burgess, R. D. McKenzie, et al., *The City* (Chicago, 1925), pp. 47–62.

2. A total of 5,009 dwellings were built in central Dorchester during the years 1872–1901. This area included 22.4 percent of all the residential building in the study area. For the location of each dwelling and statistical summaries, see Warner, "Residential Development," Atlas and Appendix F.

3. This railroad underwent several changes of name. It began in 1855 as the New York Central, changed to the Boston, Hartford, and Erie, then to the New York and New England, and finally was incorporated into the New York, New Haven, and Hartford Railroad. To avoid confusion with the present New York Central Railroad the name New York and New England has been used here.

4. Geographic influence: "Massachusetts Town Maps, 1831–1839" (atlas of photostats in the Massachusetts State Library, Boston); G. Morgan Hopkins, *Atlas of the County of Suffolk, Massachusetts* (Philadelphia, 1873–4), II, III, V, Bromley, *Atlas of Boston;* U. S. Geological Survey, *Boston South Quadrangle* (Washington, 1947).

5. The predominance of single- and two-family houses can be observed by walking through the district, and it appears in the estimates of structure type and in the concentration of five- to eight-room suites in ward 24 given in Massachusetts Bureau of Statistics of Labor, "Tenement House Census," *Twenty-second and Twenty-third Annual Reports, Public Document no. 15,* 2 vols., Boston, 1892–1893. Statistics analyzed in Warner, "Residential Development," Appendix B, 9, 12.

6. For further discussion of land costs see Warner, "Residential Development," Appendix D, and Phelps, *South End Factory Operatives*, pp. 31–41.

7. A good example of 1880 lower middle class houses located some distance from the center of the city can be seen just off Harrison Square at Greenwich and Orchardfield streets, Dorchester. For a biographical sketch of the subdivider, Samuel B. Pierce, see Warner, "Residential Development," pp. 80–81.

8. The Workingmen's Building Association closed out a subdivision it had been developing with single- and two-family houses by selling off the odd lots to a speculator

who built three-deckers. The subdivision included Homes avenue, Holiday and Oakley streets, near Geneva avenue, Dorchester. Suffolk Deeds Liber 2156, folio 193. For the history of one subdivision see Warner, "Residential Development," pp. 95–102.

9. For the purposes of this study the rent of $3.50 per month per room has been taken as the boundary between ordinary and premium space.

10. The proportion of first and second generation foreign born living in the study area increased by 5.6 percent during the years 1880–1905; in Boston as a whole it increased by 7.7 percent. For additional statistics see Warner, "Residential Development." Appendix A, pp. 13–14, 16–17, 19, 20–24.

11. Hopkins, *Atlas of the County of Suffolk*, III. Estate of William Gray, Jr.: plan, Suffolk Deeds, L. 1770, f. 168; covenants L. 1883, f. 353–4.

12. Building Permit no. 157, 1880. *Boston Transcript,* November 12, 1901, p. 7; January 31, 1927, p. 11.

13. Robert H. Lord, John E. Sexton, and Edward T. Harrington, *History of the Archdiocese of Boston, 1604–1943* (New York, 1944); Woods and Kennedy, "The Zone of Emergence," chapter on Dorchester.

14. No outstanding features for central Dorchester show up in the Census statistics of ward 24, 1875–1895, or for ward 20, 1895 on. In 1895 ward 20 had a slightly higher proportion of Irish than the new ward 24 and a slightly lesser proportion of Canadians. In other respects central Dorchester appears as a mixed community much like the outer part of the town and much like West Roxbury and Roxbury highlands. Under these circumstances the history of the parish of St. Peter's and a comparison of the structures built in the district with those elsewhere remains the essential evidence of this ethnic cluster's history. Susan L. Emery, *A Catholic Stronghold and Its Making: A History of St. Peter's Parish, Dorchester, etc.* (Boston, 1910), pp. 15–78; for statistical presentations see Warner, "Residential Development," Appendix A, pp. 14, 22, 24, Appendix B, pp. 10, 12.

15. For the purposes of this book the mile square of Roxbury from Washington street to Blue Hill avenue, from Dudley street to Franklin Park, has been called Roxbury highlands. In the 1870's the hilly character of this part of town lent all of Roxbury the temporary name of Boston highlands.

The remainder of Roxbury has been lumped together under the name lower Roxbury to distinguish it from West Roxbury and Roxbury highlands. Only relatively small amounts of building went on in the Back Bay parts of Roxbury during the nineteenth century, principally on the streets off Massachusetts avenue. Therefore, for all practical purposes, lower Roxbury comprises all the former town excepting the highlands and the large Back Bay tract west of Huntington avenue.

16. The building permits give the following totals for dwelling structures in the various divisions of Roxbury used in this chapter: Roxbury highlands, 2,563 dwellings, 11.5 percent of the total residential construction of the study area, 1872–1901; Tremont street district, 3,960 dwellings, 17.7 percent of total construction; remainder of lower Roxbury, 1,981 dwellings, 8.8 percent of total construction; all of Roxbury, 8,504 dwellings, 38.0 percent of total construction.

17. For discussion of six builders who were caught in financial difficulties see Warner, "Residential Development," p. 46.

18. The author's analysis of the "Tenement House Census" shows wards 19, 20, and 22 in lower Roxbury to have had 7,703 structures. There were 4,381 multiple dwellings and 3,322 singles. Of these 53.4 percent of the singles and 12.6 percent of the multiple structures had resident owners. The building habits of a representative

sample of 361 builders and 122 of the largest builders indicates that local landlordism must have been a very common pattern for rental units.

This analysis included only 60–80 percent of the rental units so that many small suites of one and two rooms were omitted. If these rentals were included probably two thirds of the total dwelling units of the area would appear in multiple structures.

19. Attack on the three-decker: Elmer S. Forbes, "Rural and Suburban Housing," *Housing Problems in America* (Philadelphia, 1912), II, 121–128; the best that can be said for the previous row housing: Charles Bernard, "A Hundred Thousand Homes," *Scribner's Monthly*, 11:477–487 (February, 1876); conversions of row houses: Wolfe, *The Lodging House Problem in Boston*, pp. 34–37; West End tenements: Porter, *Sanitary Inspection*.

20. From 1885 on, fire regulations required brick construction in all of Roxbury below the Ruggles and Ward street line. This part of lower Roxbury therefore continued in row housing of the old kind long after such practice had been abandoned elsewhere. City of Boston, *Revised Ordinances of 1892* (Boston, 1892), pp. 99–100.

21. Drake, *The Town of Roxbury*, pp. 103, 319–346, 379; Committee in Favor of the Union of Boston and Roxbury, *Report* (Boston, 1851), pp. 3–5, 14.

22. Lord, Sexton, and Harrington, *History of the Archdiocese of Boston*, II, 271; III, 251–258. Rev. John F. Byrne, *The Glories of Mary in Boston* (Boston, 1921), pp. 42–3, 135–144, 391–393. Woods and Kennedy, "The Zone of Emergence," chapters on Roxbury.

23. Sanitary survey of the district: Mass. Bureau of Statistics of Labor, *Twenty-third Annual Report, Mass. Public Document no. 15* (Boston, 1893); Husc, *The Financial History of Boston*, pp. 266–268.

24. For nationality statistics see Warner, "Residential Development," Appendix A, pp. 22, 24.

25. Suffolk Deeds, L. 1635, f. 231–233.

26. The preceding analysis of the interaction between building and the economic history of a neighborhood is taken from the contemporary observations of Woods and Kennedy, "The Zone of Emergence," chapters on Roxbury.

27. Robert Treat Paine (1835–1910): obituary by Robert A. Woods, *Boston Transcript*, August 12, 1910, p. 7; Robert T. Paine, "Homes for the People," *Journal of Social Science*, 15:1–19 (September, 1881); Paine, "Housing Conditions of Boston," *Annals of the American Academy of Political and Social Science*, 3:121–136 (July, 1902).

28. Examples of plans and financial terms: Ruggles street (now replaced by a federal housing project), Suffolk Deeds, L. 1189, f. 117, 170 and L. 1888, f. 385; Greenwich, Warwick, and Sussex streets (many still standing), Suffolk Deeds, L. 1762, f. 177 and L. 1765, f. 597–598; Building Permits nos. 255–284, 1886.

29. U. S. Commissioner of Labor, *Eighth Special Report, The Housing of the Working People* (Washington, 1895), pp. 200–211; *American Architect and Building News*, January 20, June 16, July 28, 1877, pp. 19–21, 185, 237; Charles Bernard, "A Hundred Thousand Homes," *Scribner's Monthly*, 11:477–487; Alfred T. White, *Improved Dwellings for the Laboring Classes* (New York, 1879); James Hole, *The Homes of the Working Classes with Suggestions for their Improvement* (London, 1866).

30. Purchase and subdivision plan: Suffolk Deeds, L. 1826, f. 569; L. 1844, f. 161. Examples of individual sales: Suffolk Deeds, L. 1861, f. 424; L. 2011, f. 520; L. 2027, f. 252; Building Permits, nos. 1217–1232, 1890. Similar Dorchester undertaking: Oakley street, Suffolk Deeds, L. 2156, f. 192; L. 2308, f. 97; Building Permits nos. 785–788, 1894.

31. For occupational and ethnic statistics see Warner, "Residential Development," Appendix A, pp. 13–14, 21–24.

32. All Souls (Roxbury) Unitarian Church: *The Roxbury Magazine* (Boston, 1899), pp. 36–38; Richard W. Hale, Jr., *Tercentenary History of the Roxbury Latin School* (Cambridge, 1946), pp. 120–147; Thomas Gray, Jr., *Change, A Poem Pronounced at Roxbury, Oct. 8, 1830, in Commemoration of the First Settlement of That Town* (Roxbury, 1830).

33. Lord, Sexton, and Harrington, *History of the Archdiocese of Boston*, III, 251–255.

34. Drake, *Town of Roxbury*, pp. 230–232, 377. William A. Crafts, *Forest Hills Cemetery* (Roxbury, 1855). Park referenda: *Boston Transcript*, November 9, 1870, p. 4; June 10, 1875, p. 1.

35. Francis S. Drake, "Roxbury in the Last Hundred Years," *Memorial History of Boston*, III, 575–588; Arthur W. Austin, *Opening Argument on Behalf of the Jamaica Pond Aqueduct Co., etc.* (Boston, 1867), pp. 23–24; Roxbury Committee Opposed to the Annexation to Boston, *A Word for Old Roxbury* (Roxbury, 1851); and *Another Word for Old Roxbury, In Reply to the Report of the Committee in Favor of Annexation* (Boston, 1852).

36. Committee in Favor of the Union of Boston and Roxbury, *Report* (Boston, 1851); John H. Clifford, *Argument on the Question of the Annexation of Roxbury to Boston, before the Legislative Committee, Thursday, February 23, 1865* (Boston, 1867).

37. For rental statistics see Warner, "Residential Development."

CHAPTER SIX. REGULATION WITHOUT LAWS

1. The general analysis of banking and finance in this chapter is an extension of the logic set forth in Bray Hammond, *Banking and Politics in America from the Revolution to the Civil War* (Princeton, N. J., 1957), espec. pp. 671–717.

2. Some idea of what constituted a good conservative investment may be gathered from the changing investments authorized for Massachusetts Savings Banks. In general, the trend of the regulatory statutes was from limitation to local mortgages toward permission to own national utility bonds. John T. Croteau, "The Development of Mutual Savings Banks in Massachusetts" (unpubl. diss., Clark University, 1935), pp. 245–246. For lower middle class investment habits and their effect upon home ownership see Phelps, *The South End Factory Operatives*, pp. 32–42.

3. The *Boston Transcript* devoted a daily column to real estate affairs, publishing the day's building permits and important transfers of property. Nearby, often on the same page, appeared the columns of advertisements of mortgage brokers and real estate dealers.

4. A special U. S. Census study of 1890, *Eleventh Census*, XV, 424, 504, 534, indicates that both in Boston and in the nation as a whole 86 percent of all home mortgages carried from 5–6 percent interest. Boston and Cambridge owners estimated the percentage of their mortgage to the value of their home to be 48 percent; the national average was 69 percent. Although the legal maximum for Massachusetts Savings Banks was 60 percent, no deed was found that showed a mortgage load in excess of 40 percent.

Many of the active real estate dealers specialized in second mortgages—Samuel B. Pierce, Suffolk Deeds, Grantor Index, 1800–1899; often successful first mortgages were assigned to banks—Charles and Cheever Newhall, Suffolk Deeds, Grantor Index, 1800–1899.

5. Cooperative banks and building societies pioneered in the writing of amortizing mortgages but their share of the total home mortgage market was small, U. S. Commissioner of Labor, *Ninth Annual Report* (Washington, 1894), pp. 300–301, 318.

6. For discussion of tenure see Warner, "Residential Development," Appendix D.

7. Of the dozens of mortgages looked at in the course of subdivision research in the Suffolk Deeds, very few were found to have been held by parties living beyond the Boston metropolitan region. Among the 122 most active builders only one, Peter Graffam of Malden, was known never to have lived in the study area or Boston.

8. The example given in the text is a generalized composite of subdivision behavior. A complete account of one subdivision is given in Warner, "Residential Development," pp. 95–102. Another good example from the Ashmont section of Dorchester: estate of Walter Baker and Roswell Gleason, Suffolk Deeds, L. 2007, f. 483; L. 2067, f. 611; L. 2220, f. 362.

9. For information on the popularity and usefulness of straws the author is indebted to Mr. Roswell G. Hall, 44 Tremlett street, Dorchester. Mr. Hall was an active mortgage broker in the district.

10. Henry E. Foley, *Special Laws of the Commonwealth of Massachusetts Relating to the City of Boston* (Boston, 1938), I, 86 (Ch. 236 of 1845); Matthews, *The City Government of Boston,* pp. 82–96; Huse, *The Financial History of Boston* pp. 260–264.

11. One may contrast covenanted and uncovenanted development by comparing the mixed building of the 1880 streets to the south of Washington and Harvard streets, Dorchester, with the more uniform convenanted streets of the 1890's in the Ashmont section, farther down Washington. Examples of Ashmont covenants: Carruth, Fairfax, and Beaumont streets, Suffolk Deeds, L. 1608, f. 233; Wellesley Park, L. 2547, f. 287–288 and L. 3439, f. 324. Back Bay covenant tradition: height, placement, and use restrictions, Suffolk Deeds, L. 933, f. 55; L. 1745, f. 218, 221. For suburban covenants: limited time, set-back restriction, L. 1874, f. 140; L. 2210, f. 289; no liquor manufacture or sale, without limit of time, L. 1863, f. 612; no three-deckers, L. 2295, f. 323; no fences, L. 1849, f. 201; minimum price of house, L. 2547, f. 287–288; single-family house only, L. 3439, f. 324.

12. For the size of parcels and ownership see Hopkins, *Atlas of the County of Suffolk,* II, III, V; Bromley, *Atlas of Boston.*

13. For more discussion of Whitney's Brookline project see Warner, "Residential Development," pp. 68–74. The revival in the twentieth century of the large-scale project "The Heights" (R. T. Paine) in Revere: Suffolk Deeds, L. 2198, end.

14. For a list of the 122 most active builders, date and place of birth, location and amount of building, and lists of occupations, see Warner, "Residential Development," Appendix B.

The places of birth were discovered for 59 of the 122 most active builders. These were distributed as follows: study area and Boston, 12; other Massachusetts, 3 rural, 2 urban; New Hampshire, 5; Maine, 9; Rhode Island, 3 rural; Vermont, 3; Maritime Provinces, 13; New York, 1 rural; New Jersey, 1 rural; Scotland, 2; Ireland, 3; Switzerland, 1 urban; total, 44 rural, 15 urban.

A contemporary study indicates that the dominance of the Maritimes in the building trades was general throughout Boston, Frederick A. Bushee, "Ethnic Factors in the Population of Boston," *Publications of the American Economic Association,* 4:80–83 (Third Series, New York, May, 1903).

15. *American Architect and Building News,* March 24, June 2, 1877, pp. 94–5, 170.

16. Popular taste: Clarence Cook, "Beds and Tables, Stools and Candlesticks," Scribner's Monthly, 11:342–357 (January 1876); George L. Hersey, "Godey's Choice," *Journal of the Society of Architectural Historians,* 18:104–111 (October 1959). Builders' books: John Bullock, *The American Cottage Builder* (New York, 1854); Amos J. Bicknell, *Wooden and Brick Buildings* (New York, 1875), 2 vols.; George E. Woodward,

Suburban and Country Houses (New York, 1873); *Woodward's National Architect* (New York, 1869 and 1877), 2 vols.; Henry-Russell Hitchcock, *American Architectural Books* (Minneapolis, 1946).

17. The lineage of Boston's grid street and frontage lot system: Elisabeth M. Herlihy, "The History of Boston's Street System," *Report on a Thoroughfare Plan for Boston* (Robert Whitten ed., Boston Planning Board, Boston, 1930), pp. 150–169; Whitehill, *A Topographical History*, pp. 22–94. North and West End: Robert A. Woods, ed., *Americans in Process* (Boston, 1903), pp. 32–44. South End: Robert A. Woods, ed., *The City Wilderness* (Boston, 1898), chap. 2.

18. Boston subdividers were successful in keeping their share of the costs down and shifting a good deal of the development expense onto the general taxpayer. In Dorchester a state representative who tried to reverse this policy was defeated for re-election. Rep. Joseph I. Stewart, *Boston Transcript*, October 30, 1899, p. 5; Huse, *Financial History of Boston*, pp. 307–309. The anger of a mayor against suburban landowners: Matthews, *City Government of Boston*, pp. 85, 92, 175.

19. Matthews, *City Government of Boston*, pp. 82–92.

20. In the study area the principal sanitary exception concerned lower Roxbury and the periodic floods of Stony Brook. In an attempt to keep this land permanently dry the city was forced to spend $2,500,000 by 1900. Roxbury City Missionary, quoted in The Committee in Favor of the Union of Boston and Roxbury, *Report* (Boston, 1851), p. 14; Huse, *Financial History of Boston*, pp. 266–267.

21. See Brookline avenue, Cedar street, and Linwood park, Roxbury, in Hopkins, *Atlas of the County of Suffolk*, II.

22. The general architectural movement known as the "picturesque" began in Europe in the eighteenth century and covered a whole host of styles from Indian to Gothic. The most popular styles around suburban Boston were the romantic-classical varieties, first the Greek Revival, and then in the 1850's the Italianate styles of Andrew J. Downing's *Cottage Residences* (New York, 1844). This latter style with its heavy baroque ornament continued to be used well into the 1870's until it was driven from the field by shingle adaptations of Richardson's work. The only important exception to this outline was the vogue of the Second Empire which produced in the 1860's, rows and rows of mansard houses both in the South End and Roxbury, and even in more distant places. The Panic of 1873 and perhaps the defeat of France in the Franco-Prussian War seems to have brought a sudden collapse of the fashion in 1873. Henry-Russell Hitchcock, *Architecture in the 19th and 20th Centuries* (Baltimore, 1958), 92–114, 152–172.

23. The preceeding architectural outline is taken from Vincent J. Scully, *The Shingle Style* (New Haven, 1955), pp. 71–112, 126–164.

CHAPTER SEVEN. THE CONSEQUENCES

1. *Boston Transcript*, March 6, 1893, p. 1.

2. Josiah Quincy, *Moderate Houses for Moderate Means, A Letter to Rev. E. E. Hale* (Boston, 1874); Woods and Kennedy, "The Zone of Emergence," chapters on Dorchester and Roxbury.

3. Even the most active municipal government in the metropolitan region, the City of Boston, undertook to deal with a rather narrow range of subject matter in its municipal affairs. Matthews, *The City Government* of Boston, pp. 174–182; Quincy, *The Development of American Cities*.

The limitation of municipal subject matter was reflected in the city's expenditure patterns: in the period 1868–1871 Boston spent 62.0 percent of its budget on real estate affairs (water, sewers, streets, and public grounds); in the period 1883–1886, 50.4 percent; in the period 1903–1906, 52.2 percent (included rapid transit). Huse, *The Financial History of Boston,* p. 366.

4. Contemporary recognition of the problem of the scale of governmental units: Sylvester Baxter, *Greater Boston; A Study for a Federated Metropolis* (Boston, 1891); Massachusetts Metropolitan Commission, *Report to the Massachusetts Legislature* (Boston, 1896), pp. 17–19, 33–34.

5. Woods and Kennedy, "The Zone of Emergence," chapters on Roxbury and Dorchester; Wolfe, *The Lodging House Problem,* pp. 1–26, 34–37.

6. One of the basic attempts of the nineteenth century settlement house movement was to discover the facts of the existence of "the other half." In Boston, the first fruit of this effort was Woods, *The City Wilderness* (1898). The title meant to convey both a sense of social disintegration and the fact that to middle class Bostonians this was an unknown land. The same tone follows through all this group's work, *Americans in Process* (1903), and "The Zone of Emergence" (c. 1912). For the general reform background: Arthur Mann, *Yankee Reformers in an Urban Age* (Cambridge, 1954), espec. 126–200.

7. Boston City Council and Roxbury City Council, *Reports in Relation to the Annexation of Roxbury, etc.,* Roxbury City Document no. 3 (Boston, 1867); John H. Clifford, *Argument on the Question of the Annexation of Roxbury to Boston before the Legislative Committee, Thursday, February 23, 1865* (Boston, 1867); Nathaniel W. Coffin, *A Few Reasons in Favor of the Annexation of a Part of the Town of Dorchester to the City of Boston* (Boston, 1867); Committee in Favor of the Union of Boston and Roxbury, *Report* (Boston, 1851).

8. Josiah Quincy, Sr., *Annexation of Roxbury and Boston. Remonstrance of Bostonians against the Measure* (Boston, 1865); *Considerations Respectfully Submitted to the Citizens of Boston and Charlestown on the Proposed Annexation of the Two Cities* (Boston, 1851); Arthur W. Austin, *Address at the Dedication of the Town-House at Jamaica Plain, West Roxbury* (Boston, 1860); Rufus Choate, *Speech on Application of Samuel D. Bradford and Others To Set Off Wards 6, 7, & 8 of the City of Roxbury as a Separate Agricultural Town* (Boston, 1851); B. W. Harris, *The Annexation Question, Closing Argument for the Remonstrants Against the Annexation of Dorchester to Boston . . .* (Boston, 1869); Roxbury Committee Opposed to the Annexation to Boston, *A Word for Old Roxbury* (Roxbury, 1851), *Another Word for Old Roxbury, In Reply to the Report of the Committee in Favor of Annexation* (Boston, 1852); Alfred D. Chandler, *Annexation of Brookline to Boston* (Brookline, 1880), pp. 15, 18.

9. Review of the whole late nineteenth and early twentieth century metropolitan government movement, a movement that was always alive but never in danger of being achieved: Joseph H. Beale, "The Metropolitan District," *Fifty Years of Boston* (Elisabeth M. Herlihy ed., Boston, 1932), pp. 116–127. Complete bibliography of the metropolitan and annexation pamphlet literature: Katherine McNamara, *The Boston Metropolitan District* (Cambridge, 1946).

10. Loss of Boston's home rule: Henry Parkman, Jr., "The City and the State, 1880–1930," *Fifty Years of Boston,* pp. 128–147.

INDEX

Atheneum Paperbacks

HISTORY—AMERICAN

Atheneum Paperbacks

STUDIES IN AMERICAN NEGRO LIFE

Atheneum Paperbacks

HISTORY

HISTORY—ASIA

Atheneum Paperbacks

THE NEW YORK TIMES BYLINE BOOKS

CHINA *by Harry Schwartz*
RUSSIA *by Harrison E. Salisbury*
THE MIDDLE EAST *by Jay Walz*
AFRICA *by Waldemar A. Nielsen*
LATIN AMERICA *by Tad Szulc*
SOUTHEAST ASIA *by Tillman Durdin*

THE ADAMS PAPERS

TAP   THE ADAMS PAPERS: DIARY AND AUTOBIOGRAPHY OF JOHN ADAMS
1,2,3,4   *edited by L. H. Butterfield, 4 vols.*
TAP   THE ADAMS PAPERS: ADAMS FAMILY CORRESPONDENCE *edited by*
5,6   *L. H. Butterfield, 2 vols.*
TAP   THE ADAMS PAPERS: DIARY OF CHARLES FRANCIS ADAMS *edited by*
7,8   *L. H. Butterfield, 2 vols.*
TAP   THE ADAMS PAPERS: LEGAL PAPERS OF JOHN ADAMS *edited by*
9,10,11   *L. H. Butterfield, 3 vols.*

ECONOMICS AND BUSINESS

21   BIG BUSINESS LEADERS IN AMERICA *by W. Lloyd Warner and James Abegglen*
24   PROSPERITY AND DEPRESSION *by Gottfried Haberler*
34   THE DIPLOMACY OF ECONOMIC DEVELOPMENT *by Eugene R. Black*
47   ECONOMIC CONCENTRATION AND THE MONOPOLY PROBLEM
     by Edward S. Mason
78   THE ECONOMICS OF DEFENSE IN THE NUCLEAR AGE *by Charles J. Hitch and Roland N. McKean*
80   FOUNDATIONS OF ECONOMIC ANALYSIS *by Paul Anthony Samuelson*
86   THE CORPORATION IN MODERN SOCIETY *edited by Edward S. Mason*

Atheneum Paperbacks

LAW AND GOVERNMENT

DIPLOMACY AND INTERNATIONAL RELATIONS

Atheneum Paperbacks

TEMPLE BOOKS—*The Jewish Publication Society*

PHILOSOPHY AND RELIGION

Atheneum Paperbacks

Atheneum Paperbacks

THE WORLDS OF NATURE AND MAN

LITERATURE AND THE ARTS